ROCK LYRICS QUIZ BOOK

Presley Love

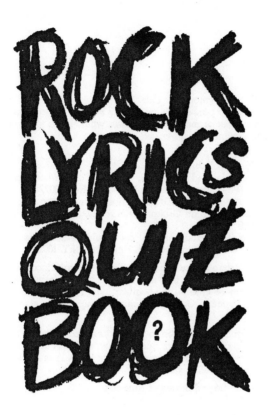

ROCK LYRICS QUIZ BOOK?

A CITADEL PRESS BOOK
Published by Carol Publishing Group

A Citadel Press Book
Published by Carol Publishing Group
Citadel Press is a registered trademark of Carol Communications, Inc.
Editorial Offices: 600 Madison Avenue, New York, N.Y. 10022
Sales and Distribution Offices: 120 Enterprise Avenue, Secaucus, N.J. 07094
In Canada: Canadian Manda Group, P.O. Box 920, Station U, Toronto,
    Ontario M8Z 5P9
Queries regarding rights and permissions should be addressed to Carol
Publishing Group, 600 Madison Avenue, New York, N.Y. 10022

Carol Publishing Group books are available at special discounts for bulk
purchases, sales promotions, fund-raising, or educational purposes.
Special editions can be created to specifications. For details, contact
Special Sales Department, Carol Publishing Group, 120 Enterprise Avenue,
Secaucus, N.J. 07094

We encourage all readers to listen to your oldies records while perusing
this book. However, public performance of most songs is under copyright
restriction by ASCAP/BMI; extensive replication of lyrics is restricted under
copyright of the writer and/or publisher.

Manufactured in the United States of America
10 9 8 7 6 5 4 3 2

Library of Congress Cataloging-in-Publication Data

Love, Presley.
    Rock lyrics quiz book / by Presley Love.
        p.   cm.
    "A Citadel Press book."
    ISBN 0-8065-1527-9
    1. Rock music—Texts—Miscellania.   I. Title.
ML3534.L7   1994
782.42166'0268—dc20   93-46589
                                                            CIP
                                                            MN

Computer-entry: Barbara Bower

...dedicated to Pancho...

Contents

Preface

I wrote the *Rock Lyrics Quiz Book* as an exciting way to test the reader's knowledge of music, past and present. Originally released in a special 1950s–1960s version in 1992, this book is now in a much expanded format, and includes artists from the seventies, eighties, and nineties as well!

I have always believed that rock and pop music lyrics reflect the social and political values of each era, and I have tried to prove how memorable the lyrics really are by compiling this book as a tribute to the artists and the tunes that we've sung along with and believed in throughout the years.

Play some of your old records and tapes, slip in a compact disc, and groove to the *Rock Lyrics Quiz Book* while you let the music fire your imagination. It's time to really listen to what the kids have been saying, what we are all saying, even today. There's a lot more to a song than a pretty melody. Whether you're into the Beatles or Billy Joel or Pearl Jam, there are messages in their songs as profound as any you'll ever see. And in case you've become a little rusty over the years, this book will help refresh you with twelve hundred all-new questions covering the most memorable lyrics in the rock and pop world.

Let your mind wander to a land where only music exists. There's no traffic and there are no school bells, no schedules, and no deadlines. There's only sweet, sweet music crashing against the shore, inviting you to believe in the magic of rock and roll and let the sounds take you away. It's time to have a party—even if it's only a daydream—aboard your own yellow submarine. Bring your friends and your laughter, too. It's time to party to *Rock Lyrics* all night long!

How to Use the
Rock Lyrics Quiz Book

This book is divided into ten sections, each of which focuses on a specific genre or era. Quiz A contains 50 multiple-choice questions, as does Quiz B. Both quizzes are equally difficult, but you may find Quiz B a bit more challenging. The Bonus Quiz contains twenty questions, some of which should definitely stump you. They're only for the know-it-alls!

Score Yourself:

Here's a chart to see how well you *really* know your music!

Quizzes A and B
(50 questions each)

If you score...	then you...
45–50 correct	REALLY know your music! (Ph.D.)
40–44 correct	are a bona fide music enthusiast
35–39 correct	are a little rusty and need to put more music in your life
30–34 correct	have forgotten the best part of life—it's time to party
0–29 correct	need to report AT ONCE to your music store to catch up on everything you've missed

Bonus Quiz
(20 questions)

if you score...   then you...

18–20 correct   REALLY know your music (Ph.D.)
15–17 correct   are a bona fide music enthusiast
10–14 correct   could use some more grooves in your
                     life
0–9 correct   are ordered to turn on your nearest
                     radio and spend four hours per day
                     mellowing out to the music

Elvis and the Early Rockers
(1950s)

The era of rock and roll officially began with the 1955 release and subsequent success of *Rock Around the Clock* by Bill Haley and His Comets. Early rockers include Hall-of-Famers such as Chuck Berry and Buddy Holly as well as country-rock crossovers such as Johnny Cash and Carl Perkins. And let's not forget the individual who made gyrating hips a part of everyone's life: Elvis, the King. Add the do-wop sounds of the Elegants, Diamonds, and Barry Mann, and you've got a dynamic flow of sounds that had never before been heard.

QUIZ A

1. Elvis Presley doesn't want to be friends with his *Hound Dog* acquaintance because she never caught a ___.
   a. rabbit
   b. cold
   c. scent

2. In *Rock and Roll Music*, under what condition does Chuck Berry not like jazz music?
   a. if they try to change the melody
   b. when the words aren't clear
   c. if he isn't performing it

1

3. In *Mean Woman Blues (I Got a Woman)*, Roy Orbison describes her as having ___.
    a. a motor-mouth
    b. lips like cherries
    c. shapely hips

4. In *Whole Lot-ta Shakin' Goin' On*, what does Jerry Lee Lewis say they'll have in the barn?
    a. a hay loft
    b. chicken
    c. lots of sheep

5. In *Oh Boy*, what does Buddy Holly say makes everything right?
    a. your sweet kiss
    b. a little bit of lovin'
    c. when you tell him you'll always stay

6. *'Til I Kissed You*, what hadn't the Everly Brothers known?
    a. that kisses taste funny
    b. what they missed
    c. true love

7. Even if Ricky Nelson, *A Teenage Idol*, finds fortune and fame, under what condition won't it mean a thing to him?
    a. if he's all alone
    b. if love passes him by
    c. if people don't let him be free

8. When Eddie Cochran sought help from his congressman to cure the *Summertime Blues*, why didn't the official want to help him?
    a. the man didn't like the length of his hair
    b. he was too young to vote
    c. the man had his own summertime blues

9. In *Good Luck Charm*, what does Elvis Presley say no rabbit's foot can bring?
   a. money
   b. life for the rabbit
   c. happiness

10. According to Little Richard, who can't *Good Golly Miss Molly* hear calling while she's rockin' and rollin'?
    a. her mama
    b. her papa
    c. anybody

11. According to Shep and the Limelites, how long is it that *Daddy's Home*?
    a. to stay
    b. for a week
    c. until the next teardrop falls

12. In *No Particular Place to Go*, what couldn't Chuck Berry unfasten as he planned to take a stroll with his girlfriend?
    a. his seatbelt
    b. his tie
    c. her blouse

13. Besides saying *See You Later, Alligator*, Bill Haley and his Comets also add ____.
    a. see you as a wallet
    b. after awhile, crocodile
    c. but don't shed crocodile tears

14. In *(Marie's the Name of) His Latest Flame*, how does Elvis Presley describe Marie's eyes?
    a. as eyes that make men surrender
    b. as the prettiest green eyes anywhere
    c. as blue as the deepest sea

15. According to the Impalas, why is it that *I Ran All the Way Home?*
    a. someone stole my car
    b. to say I'm sorry
    c. to prove how much I love you

16. Because dreams just won't do for Roy Orbison, what does he want his *Dream Baby* to do?
    a. make his dreams come true
    b. knock on his door
    c. get out of his life

17. According to Johnny Preston, who jumped so high that he land in the *Cradle of Love?*
    a. he did
    b. Humpty Dumpty
    c. Jack

18. Elvis Presley says that the tears he shed while *Crying in the Chapel* were tears of ___.
    a. loneliness
    b. a clown
    c. joy

19. Where did Ricky Nelson, the *Travelin' Man*, walk with his pretty Polynesian baby?
    a. in the sands of Waikiki
    b. in Hong Kong
    c. to his hula hut

20. Buddy Holly's love for *Peggy Sue* is ___.
    a. based on lies
    b. rare and true
    c. never ending

21. According to the Marcels, what did the *Blue Moon* see them doing?
    a. talking to the wind
    b. smoking a reefer

c. standing alone

22. In *Don't Be Cruel,* where can you find Elvis Presley?
     a. in the school lunchroom
     b. in jail
     c. sitting all alone

23. What was Marty Robbins wearing along with *A White Sportcoat?*
     a. a pink carnation
     b. blue slacks
     c. a polka-dot tie

24. In *I Only Have Eyes for You,* what word do the Flamingos use to describe their love?
     a. exclusive
     b. limited
     c. blind

25. In *There's a Moon Out Tonight,* what do the Capris have that they never had before?
     a. a glow in their heart
     b. a sense of freedom
     c. a personality

26. What was Chuck Berry riding on when he saw *Nadine* walking in another direction?
     a. a bicycle
     b. a horse
     c. a bus

27. Although Elvis Presley says he's *A Fool Such As I,* how long does he say he'll love you?
     a. until eternity
     b. until the day he dies
     c. until the day you leave

28. According to Jimmy Dean, how tall was *Big Bad John?*
     a. 6'6"

    b. 5'10"
    c. 7'2"

29. According to Mark Dinning, what did the *Teen Angel* return to the stalled automobile on the railroad tracks to retrieve?
    a. her yearbook
    b. his high school ring
    c. the car keys

30. In *Wake Up Little Suzie*, why are the Everly Brothers and their date going to be getting home so late?
    a. they had to travel far from home
    b. Suzie fell asleep in their car
    c. they fell asleep at the movies

31. Because Elvis Presley is *Stuck on You*, what is he going to stick to you like?
    a. fly paper
    b. honey
    c. glue

32. In *Great Balls of Fire*, what does Jerry Lee Lewis do that shows how nervous he is?
    a. bite his lip
    b. twiddle his thumbs
    c. swallow his tongue

33. What does Chuck Berry's *Sweet Little Sixteen* wear to the dance?
    a. tight dresses and high-heeled shoes
    b. tennis shoes with pink shoe laces
    c. a tear-away blouse and polka-dot undies

34. In *You Are My Special Angel*, from where does Bobby Helms say you came?
    a. from his most secret dreams
    b. from a place called Love
    c. from up above

35. In *You Belong to Me*, what sites along the Nile do the Duprees say it's all right to visit?
    a. the canals
    b. the pyramids
    c. the swamps

36. In order to try to *Get a Job*, what do the Silhouettes examine carefully?
    a. the newspaper
    b. their previous job experience
    c. their future

37. In *(Let Me Be Your) Teddy Bear*, why doesn't Elvis Presley want to be a lion?
    a. they aren't loved enough
    b. they get hungry too easily
    c. they're always lyin' around

38. What happened to Johnny Cash with the *Ring of Fire*?
    a. he discovered that his life of drinking had turned him into a walking time bomb
    b. his girlfriend gave his ring away
    c. he fell into it

39. According to the Edsels, *Rama Lama Ding Dong* is the name of _____.
    a. their girlfriend
    b. a new dance
    c. their pet llama

40. When you kissed the Danleers so tenderly *One Summer Night*, what did they realize?
    a. you and they would soon get married
    b. it was all just a game
    c. this was love

41. In *Ready Teddy*, what is Little Richard ready to do?
    a. rock and roll

   b.   go home with you
   c.   make love to you

42.   When Elvis Presley says *Treat Me Nice*, he expects you to scratch his back and ___.
   a.   make him purr
   b.   rub his tummy
   c.   run your fingers through his hair

43.   In *Maybe, Baby*, what do Buddy Holly and the Crickets feel they'll have one day?
   a.   true love
   b.   you
   c.   a successful rock and roll career

44.   In *When Will I Be Loved*, what happens to the Everly Brothers every time they meet a new girl whom they want for themselves?
   a.   they find she's already married
   b.   she breaks their hearts
   c.   their hearts stop beating

45.   What is the reason Ricky Nelson says now *It's Up to You*?
   a.   he's done everything he can
   b.   he's ready to do it
   c.   he's gone down as far as a man can go

46.   What does Chuck Berry tell *Carol* that he's going to learn to do if it takes him all night and day?
   a.   love her
   b.   dance
   c.   read

47.   Why does Elvis Presley want you to *Wear My Ring Around Your Neck*?
   a.   to show the world that he's yours
   b.   so you don't lose it
   c.   so you'll remember whose girl you are

48. According to Don Gibson in *Oh, Lonesome Me,* what is everybody going out and doing?
    a. dancing
    b. throwing up
    c. having fun

49. Because his girlfriend had *Kisses Sweeter Than Wine,* what did Jimmie Rodgers do immediately after he kissed her for the first time?
    a. he proposed to her
    b. he brushed his teeth
    c. he kissed her again

50. In *Rock and Roll Is Here to Stay,* what do Danny and the Juniors say will become of rock and roll?
    a. it'll soon change to rap and soul
    b. it'll go down in history
    c. it'll be the reason everyone's happy

QUIZ B

1. When Elvis Presley asks *Are You Lonesome Tonight?* he wonders whether you gaze at your doorstep and do what?
   a. go into a trance
   b. undress him with your eyes
   c. picture him there

2. In *All I Have to Do Is Dream,* what is the only problem for the Everly Brothers?
   a. they're dreaming their life away
   b. dreams never come true
   c. they're flunking out of school

3. In *Tutti Frutti,* what is the name of Little Richard's girlfriend who drives him crazy?
   a. Mazie

    b. Daisy

    c. Anastasie

4. Roy Orbison says *Only the Lonely* must take a chance if they wish to find what?

    a. happiness

    b. heaven

    c. romance

5. How did Chuck Berry get *Back in the USA*?

    a. in a cab, past the border

    b. by plane

    c. smuggled in a trunk

6. According to Ricky Nelson in *It's Late*, what time should they have left home to have plenty of time?

    a. 7:00

    b. noon

    c. 8:45

7. In *G.I. Blues*, what is Elvis Presley going to do if he doesn't go stateside soon?

    a. blow a fuse

    b. turn gay

    c. write himself a letter

8. What do the Falcons do to celebrate how *You're So Fine*?

    a. talk about you

    b. dream about you at night

    c. say a prayer

9. Although Guy Mitchell has *Heartaches by the Number*, what does he say will happen the day he stops counting?

    a. his world will end

    b. a new love will begin

    c. he'll take algebra

10. In *I Want You, I Need You, I Love You*, what is it that Elvis Presley thought he could live without until he met you?
    a. beer
    b. romance
    c. goals

11. With whom did Marty Robbins fall in love in *El Paso*?
    a. a barroom queen
    b. a Mexican girl
    c. the bartender

12. According to Carl Dobkins, Jr. in *My Heart Is an Open Book*, who does he love?
    a. nobody
    b. everyone
    c. you

13. What do the Elegants ask the *Little Star* up above for?
    a. a break
    b. a sunny day tomorrow
    c. a love to share

14. In *Love Me Tender*, what does Elvis Presley ask you to fulfill?
    a. all his dreams
    b. his fantasies
    c. your promise to him

15. In *Believe What You Say*, what does Ricky Nelson know for sure?
    a. you're going steady with nobody else
    b. you've been lying
    c. he's never met another girl like you

16. According to Jimmie Rodgers, what was made from a million trips to the *Honeycomb?*
    a. a tone of honey
    b. his baby's lips
    c. a million dollars

17. Where do the Diamonds want you to do *The Stroll* with them?
    a. across the floor
    b. through the park
    c. past the fantasies of your mind

18. In *Walk Right Back*, what do the Everly Brothers want you to explain?
    a. why you walked out on them
    b. what the other boy offered that they didn't give
    c. why they should take you back

19. When Chuck Berry says to *Roll Over, Beethoven*, to whom does he say to tell the news?
    a. you
    b. Rover
    c. Tchaikovsky

20. What is Elvis Presley doing on the lonely back road in the *Kentucky Rain?*
    a. looking for you
    b. thumbing for a ride
    c. trying to find his way back home

21. According to Buddy Holly in *That'll Be the Day*, the day his baby says goodbye to him and makes him cry will be the day ___.
    a. he knows she loves him
    b. he says he's sorry
    c. he dies

22. When did Little Richard find that his *Lucille* was not around?
    a. last night

    b. just now

    c. this morning

23. Once Ricky Nelson said *Hello, Mary Lou,* he knew he'd said goodbye to what?

    a. his old girlfriend

    b. his freedom

    c. his heart

24. What question haunts Roy Orbison and has him *Running Scared?*

    a. Is he after you or after me?

    b. Is he related to Charles Manson?

    c. If he came back, which one would you choose?

25. Now that they have discovered they've become *Cathy's Clown,* what things don't the Everly Brothers want from her anymore?

    a. her excuses

    b. her kisses

    c. her jokes

26. The Fiestas' girlfriend is *So Fine* because she'll do what—come rain, come shine?

    a. anything they want

    b. love them

    c. never leave them

27. In Elvis Presley's *Can't Help Falling in Love,* who says that only fools rush in?

    a. those in love

    b. wise men

    c. people who've never been in love

28. What did Chuck Berry's *Johnny B. Goode* use to carry his guitar inside of?

    a. a guitar case

    b. a gunnysack

    c. a paper bag

29. According to Bill Haley and his Comets in *Shake, Rattle and Roll*, even with your hair done up so nice, how are you deep inside?
    a. cold as ice
    b. shy as a teenage queen
    c. playful like a tomboy

30. In *Blue Suede Shoes*, what does Carl Perkins say it's OK to step on?
    a. his face
    b. his feet
    c. the hot asphalt

31. In *Bo Diddley*, what does Bo Diddley say he'll do if his diamond ring doesn't shine?
    a. trade it in for a ruby
    b. take it to a private eye
    c. buy a bottle of expensive wine

32. According to the Five Satins' *In the Still of the Night*, in which month do they remember the night's stars shining brightly above?
    a. May
    b. every month
    c. June

33. In *Return to Sender*, what happens when Elvis Presley keeps sending letters of apology to his girlfriend?
    a. she keeps tearing them up
    b. the letters keep coming back
    c. she writes him back more letters

34. How does Ricky Nelson describe the eyes of the girl who tricked him into being a *Poor Little Fool*?
    a. soft and entrancing
    b. carefree devil eyes
    c. sickly and bulging

35. In order to hide their teardrops, what kind of weather do the Everly Brothers look for in *Crying in the Rain?*
a. a typhoon
b. hail and sleet
c. a storm

36. What does Thurston Harris ask his *Little Bitty Pretty One* to come sit on, to listen to a story he wants to tell?
a. a stool
b. his bed
c. his knee

37. For Danny and the Juniors, what is the coolest *At the Hop?*
a. the drinks
b. the chicks
c. the music

38. At what hour are Bill Haley and his Comets going to have some fun in *Rock Around the Clock?*
a. 1:00 A.M.
b. midnight
c. 10:00 P.M.

39. In *Stood Up, Broken-Hearted Again,* since what time has Ricky Nelson been waiting for his date?
a. midnight
b. 3:00
c. 8:00

40. What do the Diamonds want to know from their *Little Darlin'?*
a. does she love them
b. where is she
c. is she coming over to see them

41. Although Elvis Presley says you're the *Devil in Disguise*, what does he say you do like an angel?

   a. walk

   b. enchant

   c. smile

42. In what model car was Chuck Berry's *Maybellene* riding?

   a. a super-stock Dodge

   b. a Cadillac Coupe De Ville

   c. a Nash Rambler

43. In *Everyday,* what do Buddy Holly's friends all advise him to do?

   a. find out who was with his girl last night

   b. ask to go steady

   c. look for a job

44. According to Jimmie Rodgers, what kind of life is it when you've got a wife like *Honeycomb*?

   a. a darned good life

   b. kind of a drag

   c. the sweet life

45. What does Elvis Presley say a mother doesn't need *In the Ghetto*?

   a. promises

   b. another mouth to feed

   c. more songs about the ghetto

46. Although Roy Orbison says it's hard to explain why, what can start him suddenly *Crying*?

   a. the approach of evening

   b. the thought of you

   c. the touch of your hand

47. Jewel Akens wants to tell you about *The Birds and the Bees* and the flowers and ___.

   a. the trees

    b. the breeze

    c. his dreams

48. In *Bye Bye Love*, what do the Everly Brothers say hello to?

    a. freedom

    b. emptiness

    c. happiness

49. According to Elvis Presley, how long has *A Hard-Headed Woman* been a thorn in the side of man?

    a. ever since the world began

    b. for as long as he's known you

    c. ever since her mom moved in

50. Though *You're a Thousand Miles Away,* what do the Heartbeats still have to remember you by?

    a. your love

    b. your letters

    c. memories

BONUS QUIZ

1. How hot does Elvis Presley say his *Burning Love* must be reaching?

    a. 104°

    b. 109°

    c. 1000°

2. In *Chantilly Lace*, what time does the Big Bopper's date want him to come by?

    a. 6:00 P.M.

    b. 8:00 P.M.

    c. as soon as possible

3. Why is it that Guy Mitchell says *(I Never Felt More Like) Singing the Blues?*

    a. he never thought he'd lose your love

   b. he's in a good mood for singing about blue skies

   c. disappointment has haunted all his dreams

4. In *So This Is Love*, with what do the Castells compare their life?

   a. living in paradise
   b. a roller coaster ride
   c. the tunnel of love

5. According to Johnny Preston, where have *Running Bear* and his sweetheart gone after their tragic experience in the river?

   a. to the great tepee in the sky
   b. to the happy hunting ground
   c. through the magic mirror of life

6. In Elvis Presley's *Jailhouse Rock*, what did number 47 say to number 3?

   a. if you can't find a partner, use a wooden chair
   b. I'll see you in the showers
   c. you're the cutest little jailbird

7. What famous historical figure did Johnny Horton accompany to *The Battle of New Orleans*?

   a. General Grant
   b. General Lee
   c. Colonel Jackson

8. According to Claude King, who is living atop *Wolverton Mountain*?

   a. Dracula
   b. George Wolverton
   c. Clifton Clowers

9. What is Ral Donner's relationship with *The Girl of My Best Friend*?

   a. he doesn't like her
   b. he's her big brother
   c. he's in love with her

10. Ron Holden and the Thunderbirds *Love You So* more than ___.
    a. they can say
    b. you deserve
    c. you'll ever know

11. According to the Cleftones, what is it that you stole that held all their *Heart and Soul*?
    a. their diary
    b. a kiss
    c. their love

12. In *One Broken Heart for Sale*, what does Elvis Presley ask you to excuse him for doing?
    a. holding your hand
    b. crying
    c. loving you

13. According to Sonny James, what will tell him that your *Young Love* is real?
    a. your vow
    b. one kiss
    c. your heart

14. Although *It's Only Make Believe*, Conway Twitty's prayer is that someday ___.
    a. his dream will come true
    b. it won't matter
    c. you'll care for him

15. In what chapter of *The Book of Love* do the Monotones say you tell her that you love her with all your heart?
    a. chapter three
    b. chapter two
    c. chapter one

16. Who is the *Bird Dog* whom the Everly Brothers say is trying to steal their girl?

    a. Clarence
    b. Joey
    c. Johnny

17. On what day did Jimmie Rodgers first meet the girl with blue eyes who made him realize *Oh Oh! I'm Falling in Love Again?*
    a. Saturday
    b. Tuesday
    c. Friday

18. According to Ricky Nelson, what is the only price you have to pay when you're in *Lonesome Town?*
    a. a heart full of tears
    b. your happiness
    c. all your dreams

19. In *School Day,* what course does Chuck Berry say he's hoping to pass?
    a. history
    b. science
    c. health

20. In *A Big Hunk o' Love*, Elvis Presley says he'd have everything his lucky charms can bring if you'd do what?
    a. give him your love
    b. let him come over tonight
    c. kiss him

The Beatles
(1964-1969)

No other group so influenced the development of rock and roll as did four lads who joined the first foreign invasion into America's popular music. They weren't the first group to land on its shores, but they made the loudest impact, traces of which can be seen decades later. They deserve a category all their own, for no other artists in rock and roll history ever ruled the hit charts by having songs in the No. 1, No. 2, No. 3, No. 4, and No. 5 positions in the same week. It happened in March 1964 for the Beatles.

QUIZ A

1. In *I Should Have Known Better*, when the Beatles tell you that they love you and want you to be theirs, you're going to say ___.
   a. what's on your mind
   b. hooray
   c. you love them, too

2. According to the Beatles in *She Loves You*, why does your girlfriend have a change of heart?
   a. she knows you're not the hurtin' kind
   b. she saw your new Rolex
   c. she's an angel of a girl

3. In *I Feel Fine*, what does the Beatles' girlfriend tell them all the time?
   a. that she's theirs
   b. what to do
   c. how nice they sing

4. In *I Want to Hold Your Hand*, how do the Beatles say they feel when they touch you?
   a. powerful
   b. confused
   c. happy

5. Under what conditions do the Beatles say *You're Gonna Lose That Girl*?
   a. if you don't take her out tonight
   b. if you don't whisper sweet words of love to her
   c. if you don't shave your mustache

6. The Beatles are proud of their girlfriend because *She's a Woman* who loves ___.
   a. without reserve
   b. her man
   c. tenderly

7. In *I Saw Her Standing There*, how old was the girl the Beatles saw?
   a. seventeen
   b. thirty-four
   c. fourteen

8. In *All My Lovin'*, what will the Beatles do every day while they are away from home?
   a. telephone
   b. write home
   c. cry

9. What excuse do the Beatles give as to why *I'll Follow the Sun*?
   a. because tomorrow may rain

   b.   it's getting too hot for them there
   c.   they're afraid of the night

10. As the Beatles write their letter in *P.S. I Love You*, what do they ask you to always remember?
   a.   that they'll soon write again to you
   b.   their address and phone number
   c.   that they'll always be in love with you

11. In *Do You Want to Know a Secret*, what do the Beatles say you'll never know?
   a.   how many other girlfriends they have
   b.   the way to satisfy their heart
   c.   how much they really care

12. In *Something*, the Beatles are attracted to their girlfriend because of what?
   a.   the way she walks
   b.   the way she moves
   c.   her smile

13. In *It Won't Be Long*, although you left them, what are the Beatles happy about?
   a.   your sister likes them, too
   b.   you're coming home
   c.   they don't miss you anymore

14. Although the Beatles say in *Money* that the best things in life are free, what do they also add?
   a.   you can give them to the birds and bees
   b.   they can't buy love
   c.   it proves you don't need money

15. Although the Beatles say *Can't Buy Me Love*, what would they buy for you if it would make you feel all right?
   a.   a dog
   b.   a diamond ring
   c.   a penthouse

16. What do the Beatles want their dance partner to do when they *Twist and Shout* a little bit closer?
    a. slowly unbutton her shirt
    b. let them know that she's theirs
    c. move toward the exit

17. What is it that the Beatles get *Eight Days a Week*?
    a. love
    b. complaining
    c. fan support

18. Because the Beatles say *I Don't Want to Spoil the Party*, what do they decide to do?
    a. have a party of their own
    b. go home
    c. take a walk

19. What *Words of Love* do the Beatles hear from their sweetheart?
    a. come softly to me
    b. darling, I love you
    c. take out the trash

20. Besides calling their teasing girlfriend a *Day Tripper*, what other expression do the Beatles use?
    a. tear-away tease
    b. Sunday driver
    c. dead-end roller

21. In *I'll Be Back*, what do the Beatles say you could have found better things to do than?
    a. get hooked on drugs
    b. go out with them
    c. break their heart

22. In *Hey Jude*, the Beatles urge Jude to take a sad song and ___.
    a. make it better
    b. throw it away
    c. add a backbeat to it

23. In *Ticket to Ride*, why are the Beatles feeling that they are going to be sad?
    a. they're going to be leaving you for the summer
    b. the girl who drives them mad is going away
    c. they've been drafted

24. In *Love Me Do*, the Beatles want someone to love, somebody ___.
    a. new
    b. true
    c. cute

25. How many years ago do the Beatles say it was in *Sgt. Pepper's Lonely Hearts Club Band* that Sgt. Pepper taught the band to play?
    a. fourteen
    b. twenty
    c. thirty-four

26. What do the Beatles say they can do *With a Little Help From My Friends*?
    a. win
    b. sing
    c. get by

27. When the Beatles get home from *A Hard Day's Night*, you do things to them that make them feel ___.
    a. horrible
    b. all right
    c. excited

28. How tall do the Beatles feel in *You've Got to Hide Your Love Away* now that she's gone?
    a. two feet small
    b. ten feet tall
    c. microscopic

29. In *Get Back*, where do the Beatles say JoJo's home was?

    a. Tucson

    b. Albuquerque

    c. San Diego

30. When do the Beatles want you to *Come Together?*

    a. right now

    b. tonight

    c. when you feel the time's right

31. What do the Beatles say you can do *Anytime at All* and they'll come running to you?

    a. look their way

    b. wiggle your hips

    c. call

32. In *Help!* what do the Beatles say they never needed when they were younger?

    a. friends

    b. help

    c. love

33. Although the Beatles say all their troubles seemed so far away *Yesterday,* how do things look for them now?

    a. now they can see a bright, sunshiny day

    b. troubles are even further away

    c. troubles are here to stay

34. Where does the Beatles' *Long and Winding Road* lead to?

    a. your door

    b. paradise

    c. a dead end street

35. In *Let It Be*, who comes to the Beatles' aid when they are in times of trouble?

    a. Mother Mary

    b. Lady Madonna

    c. you do

36. In *Penny Lane*, what is so very strange to the Beatles when the fireman rushes in?

    a. he's wearing no clothes

    b. there's no fire to be seen

    c. he enters from the pouring rain

37. In *I've Just Seen a Face*, what can't the Beatles forget?

    a. how beautiful she looked

    b. that they're already going steady

    c. the time and place when they met her

38. Although the Beatles say they'd be with you *If I Needed Someone*, what precludes them from being with you?

    a. they're in love with someone else

    b. you've already got another guy

    c. they don't really like you

39. In *Revolution*, what do the Beatles say about those who go around carrying pictures of Chairman Mao?

    a. instead, they should give peace a chance

    b. they're not going to make it with anyone

    c. don't fight the feeling

40. In *And I Love Her*, the Beatles say their love will never die as long as ___.

    a. you are near them

    b. there are stars in the sky

    c. the sun keeps shining

41. In *Slow Down*, what do the Beatles say you need to give them if you want their love to last?

    a. some more time

    b. a little cash

    c. a little lovin'

42. In *You Can't Do That*, what do the Beatles say they'll do if you keep seeing other guys?
    a. cry
    b. love you even more
    c. leave you

43. In *Good Day Sunshine*, why is it a sunny day for the Beatles?
    a. they're in love
    b. you've come back to them
    c. it's the weekend

44. In *If I Fell*, what do the Beatles ask in return?
    a. if you'd promise to be true
    b. whether you'd fall in love with them
    c. if you'd like to pick them up

45. What do the Beatles ask if you'll still do *When I'm Sixty-Four*?
    a. call them
    b. feed them
    c. love them

46. Seeing children at the feet of *Lady Madonna*, what thought do the Beatles ponder?
    a. where their father is
    b. how she manages to make ends meet
    c. why she doesn't pick them up

47. In *From Me to You*, what do the Beatles say they have that's so true?
    a. their promise
    b. love
    c. a heart

48. Because they're so *Happy Just to Dance With You*, what do the Beatles suggest doing if somebody tries to take their place?
    a. tell

    b. dance

    c. pretend

49. What weren't the Beatles aware of *'Til There Was You?*

    a. paradise

    b. birds

    c. heartache

50. According to the Beatles in *I'm Looking Through You,* what has a habit of disappearing overnight?

    a. devotion

    b. love

    c. their money

QUIZ B

1. In *I Want to Be Your Man,* what do the Beatles want you to tell them?

    a. that you'll understand

    b. how to win your love

    c. if they can have this dance

2. The Beatles say in *If I Fell* that they've found out love is more than simply doing what?

    a. making promises

    b. holding hands

    c. wishing and hoping

3. In *I Need You,* what is it that you told the Beatles as they looked into your eyes?

    a. they need Visine

    b. you don't want their lovin' anymore

    c. they're the one for you, too

4. In *Don't Bother Me,* the Beatles say they'll never be the same if they don't do what?

    a. get piece of mind

    b. take Ex-Lax

    c. get her back

5. In *This Boy*, what do the Beatles say the other boy won't be happy until he sees you do?

    a. love him

    b. cry

    c. become a clown

6. About what do the Beatles say *I Should Have Known Better*?

    a. that they were only telling lies

    b. that they would love everything you do

    c. than to drink and drive at the same time

7. According to the Beatles in *Eleanor Rigby*, who is writing the words of a sermon that no one will hear?

    a. Father McKenzie

    b. they are

    c. Mother Mary

8. According to the Beatles, what is the *Magical Mystery Tour* waiting to do?

    a. fade away

    b. take you away

    c. make a movie

9. Under what condition will the Beatles remember *Things We Said Today*?

    a. when they're in court with you

    b. when they see you pass them by

    c. when they're lonely

10. Although many of their friends are aboard their *Yellow Submarine*, where do the Beatles say many more of them live?

    a. one floor below

    b. next door

    c. on the surface

11. What do the Beatles want you to *Tell Me Why?*
    a. why you love them
    b. why you cry
    c. why you're not on the pill

12. On what airline did the Beatles fly *Back in the USSR?*
    a. United
    b. Russian Air
    c. BOAC

13. In *Yes It Is*, what does wearing the color red remind the Beatles of?
    a. their failures
    b. the happy moments
    c. their baby

14. What did *Rocky Raccoon* find when he returned to his room, left there to help in his time of need?
    a. money and a note of cheer
    b. a Bible
    c. a bottle of gin

15. In *All My Loving*, the Beatles say that while they're away, they'll pretend that they're ___.
    a. sleeping with you in the same bed together
    b. really not so blue
    c. kissing the lips they are missing

16. In *Something*, answering the question whether their love will continue to grow, the Beatles respond ___.
    a. of course it will
    b. as long as she's near
    c. they don't know

17. What does the baby at the breast of *Lady Madonna* wonder, according to the Beatles?
    a. why it feels so supple

    b. how the milk gets refilled

    c. how she manages to feed the rest

18. According to the Beatles, what does the *Nowhere Man* have command over?

    a. the world

    b. nothing

    c. his life

19. What do the Beatles call *Let It Be* words of?

    a. faith

    b. wisdom

    c. resignation

20. What is it that the Beatles don't want to change through their *Revolution*?

    a. your love for them

    b. the way they live

    c. the world

21. In *Come Together*, the Beatles say that when you hold the holy roller in your arms, you can feel his
____.

    a. disease

    b. love

    c. warmth

22. What do the Beatles want you to do that you did *The Night Before*?

    a. dance with them

    b. treat them the same way

    c. spend the night

23. In *Here, There and Everywhere*, what changed life for the Beatles?

    a. the wave of her hand

    b. seeing her

    c. love

24. What will the Beatles become if they *Act Naturally*?
    a. your man
    b. a movie star
    c. a rock

25. According to the Beatles, *It Won't Be Long* before what happens with them?
    a. they belong to you
    b. they go crazy
    c. they join the Navy

26. In *No Reply,* what were the Beatles told when they tried to telephone you?
    a. sorry, wrong number
    b. you love them, too
    c. you weren't home

27. The Beatles say *You Like Me Too Much* to do what?
    a. tell them
    b. marry them
    c. leave them

28. The Beatles want to know *What You're Doing* because they're feeling ____.
    a. blue and lonely
    b. downright horny
    c. fine and dandy

29. In *Please Please Me,* what did the Beatles say last night to their girl?
    a. she never tried to please them
    b. she's gotta choose between the two
    c. she's the best person in their life

30. Although others tell the Beatles that she's got the *Devil in Her Heart,* what do they call her?
    a. Helen Blazes

    b. an angel

    c. their little devil

31. When the Beatles say *There's a Place* they can go when they're feeling low or blue, where is this place?

    a. in your room

    b. up on the roof

    c. in their mind

32. According to the Beatles, what is *The Word*?

    a. peace

    b. the bird

    c. love

33 The Beatles say that whether there's *Rain* or sunshine, it's just ___.

    a. another day

    b. a waste of time

    c. a state of mind

34. In *Norwegian Wood*, where did the Beatles sleep that evening?

    a. in the bath

    b. on the floor

    c. in her bed

35. According to the Beatles, since when is it that *It's Getting Better*?

    a. since the day they first saw you

    b. since you went away

    c. since you'll be theirs

36. What do the Beatles recommend for you to do because *She Loves You*?

    a. make her beg like a dog

    b. apologize to her

    c. take her to a movie

37. The Beatles feel that *We Can Work It Out* and get it straight or else say ___.

    a. it's over
    b. what's on their mind
    c. goodnight

38. In *I Want to Hold Your Hand*, what one thing do the Beatles want to hear?

    a. that you don't need a diamond ring
    b. you'll let them be your man
    c. your heart beat next to theirs

39. In *You're Gonna Lose That Girl*, who do the Beatles say will be her new boyfriend?

    a. them
    b. the next boy who comes along
    c. she'll keep it a secret

40. What couldn't the Beatles do after *I Saw Her Standing There*?

    a. see straight
    b. dance with another
    c. walk straight

41. In *P.S. I Love You*, the Beatles mention that they'll be coming home again to you until ___.

    a. the day they do love
    b. the Lord calls them away
    c. the rivers flow to the sea

42. If the Beatles buy things for their girlfriend in *I Feel Fine*, what do they say they'll buy?

    a. a house with a garden
    b. diamond rings
    c. rock and roll records

43. In *She's a Woman*, the Beatles don't want presents but rather that their girlfriend give them ___.

    a. money
    b. love
    c. devotion

44. The Beatles say that *Eight Days a Week* is not enough time to show ___.
    a. they care
    b. you off
    c. their abilities

45. In *I Don't Want to Spoil the Party,* how will the Beatles feel if they find their absent girlfriend?
    a. they'll be glad
    b. suspicious
    c. they won't care

46. What reason does the Beatles' girlfriend give to explain why she has purchased a *Ticket to Ride?*
    a. her school starts next week
    b. she wants to see the whole wide world
    c. she could never be free when they were around

47. In *A Hard Day's Night,* how have the Beatles been working?
    a. with a smile on their face
    b. as if they're on vacation
    c. like a dog

48. In *Paperback Writer,* what does the son of the dirty old man in the Beatles' paperback want to become?
    a. a teacher
    b. a paperback writer
    c. a rock and roll star

49. In *Help!* what do the Beatles want you to help them get back on the ground?
    a. their airplane
    b. their nose
    c. their feet

50. What did the Beatles do that makes them long for *Yesterday?*
   a. they moved away
   b. they said something wrong
   c. they let you stray

BONUS QUIZ

1. Who do the Beatles want to have join them to say *You've Got to Hide Your Love Away?*
   a. everyone
   b. all those in love
   c. all the clowns

2. In *Paperback Writer,* who is the author of the novel upon which the Beatles' book is based?
   a. Lear
   b. Starr
   c. Lane

3. What do the Beatles say you should do if you want them to send anything with love *From Me to You?*
   a. call on them
   b. just ask
   c. send them a self-addressed stamped envelope

4. In *'Til There Was You,* what appeared for the Beatles in sweet fragrant meadows of dawn?
   a. you
   b. love
   c. roses

5. According to the Beatles in *Here, There and Everywhere,* what does it mean to love a girl?
   a. to be true
   b. to need her everywhere
   c. to close your eyes to everything else

6. When the Beatles think of things they did *The Night Before*, what does it make them want to do?
   a. do it all over again
   b. call you up
   c. cry

7. In *Don't Bother Me*, what do the Beatles say she'll always be for them?
   a. the only girl
   b. a runaround flirt
   c. an impossible dream

8. In *Roll Over Beethoven*, what warning do the Beatles give?
   a. not to step on their shoes
   b. not to drink and drive
   c. not to fight their love

9. In *Rock and Roll Music*, the Beatles say they're in no mood to do which dance?
   a. the frug
   b. the twist
   c. the mambo

10. In *A Day in the Life*, who won the war in the film the Beatles saw today?
    a. the British
    b. the USA
    c. nobody won

11. In *Yes It Is*, what color don't the Beatles want you to wear tonight?
    a. black
    b. red
    c. green

12. In *Act Naturally*, what will the movie the Beatles act in be about?
    a. a teenage millionaire

    b. a writer of paperbacks
    c. a sad and lonely man

13. In *We Can Work It Out,* what do the Beatles feel is a necessary ingredient to tell who is right or wrong?
    a. compromise
    b. time
    c. love

14. Although the Beatles received *No Reply,* how did they know you were home?
    a. they saw you walk in your door
    b. they saw the silhouettes on the shade
    c. they could hear you breathing

15. The Beatles want to know *What You're Doing* ___.
    a. tomorrow
    b. to them
    c. on the phone

16. In *Please Please Me,* what do the Beatles say you don't need them to do?
    a. give you money
    b. show you the way
    c. dress in drag

17. *Back in the USSR,* girls from which area really knock the Beatles out and leave the Western girls far behind?
    a. Georgia
    b. Siberia
    c. Ukraine

18. According to the Beatles, what did *Maxwell's Silver Hammer* do?
    a. build a house for two
    b. kill people
    c. decorate the living room wall

19. In *The Ballad of John and Yoko* what do the Beatles say will happen to the guru duo the way things are going?

   a. they'll be crucified

   b. they'll have to leave the country

   c. they'll cause the group to split

20. What do the Beatles say will happen *Across the Universe?*

   a. there'll be birds chirping from the trees

   b. a new world will come

   c. nothing is going to change their world

Rhythm and Blues / Soul
(1950s-1990s)

While rock and roll highlighted the swinging beat of fast-paced bands, rhythm and blues told a different story in a different way. Early stars such as Little Anthony and the Imperials and Fats Domino attracted a diverse following, creating a new dimension to the rock experience. The R and B flavor evolved into "soul," aided greatly by Motown groups such as Smokey Robinson and the Miracles and the Supremes. Even today, groups such as Boyz II Men and Soul II Soul continue to pass along the legacy of the original R and B masters, while stars such as D.J. Jazzy Jeff and the Fresh Prince have opted to limit the musical accompaniment but still keep the beat in the hip-hop, word-oriented genre of rap. The R and B feeling is still there, only the style is being modified to change with the times.

QUIZ A

1. In *Da Doo Ron Ron*, what day did the Crystals meet Bill?
   a. Friday
   b. Monday
   c. Saturday

2. Where is the *Dock of the Bay* on which Otis Redding is sitting?
   a. San Francisco
   b. Los Angeles
   c. New York

3. The Ronettes say that, if you'll *Be My Baby,* for every kiss you give them they'll give you ___.
   a. ten
   b. three
   c. a smack

4. What was the name of Stevie Wonder's childhood sweetheart in *I Was Made to Love Her?*
   a. Cherie
   b. Sally
   c. Suzie

5. *Under the Boardwalk* the Drifters can hear the happy sounds of a ___.
   a. little baby
   b. carousel
   c. clown

6. In *You Really Got a Hold on Me,* the Temptations want their girlfriend to ___.
   a. let them go
   b. hold them tightly
   c. show them how much love they feel

7. What do Martha and the Vandellas want *Jimmy Mack* to tell them?
   a. when he's coming back
   b. why he left them
   c. why he changed his name

8. Although Johnny Rivers's girlfriend from *The Poor Side of Town* is the best thing in his life, how does he feel she is looked upon by her other boyfriend?
   a. as a plaything

    b. as a symbol of poverty
    c. as a hand-me-down

9. The Intruders can remember in *Cowboys to Girls* when their girlfriend got her first ___.
    a. baby coach
    b. baby doll
    c. skates

10. When Gene Chandler, the *Duke of Earl*, holds his sweetheart, what position is she transformed into?
    a. his slave
    b. a duchess
    c. her royal majesty

11. In *Give Me Just a Little More Time*, who does Chairman of the Board say they owe it to for their love to grow?
    a. each other
    b. their children
    c. their pastor

12. In *Nothing But Heartaches*, when do you always leave the Supremes all alone?
    a. whenever you feel tied down
    b. after spending the night with them
    c. when they need a hand to hold

13. According to the Four Tops in *Baby I Need Your Loving*, what do some people say it's a sign of weakness to do?
    a. stop eating
    b. beg
    c. apologize

14. In *It's Too Late to Turn Back Now*, what are Cornelius Brothers and Sister Rose afraid of?
    a. they're being followed
    b. they're in love alone
    c. they're going to run out of gas

15. What do the Commodores say legendary stars such as Marvin Gaye and Jackie Wilson have now found on the *Nightshift*?
    a. a permanent job
    b. peace of mind
    c. another home

16. In *Let's Stay Together*, how do you make Al Green feel?
    a. like a fool
    b. brand new
    c. insecure

17. In *Beechwood 4-5789*, what are the Marvelettes waiting so patiently for?
    a. you to come over
    b. the postman to deliver a letter
    c. a telephone call

18. What year was the car Wilson Pickett bought for *Mustang Sally*?
    a. 1952
    b. 1965
    c. 1962

19. Aretha Franklin tells her man that he had better *Think* about ___.
    a. what he is trying to do to her
    b. his future plans
    c. paying next month's rent

20. Although it is *Just My Imagination*, what do the Temptations hope to have in the country?
    a. the chance to clear their mind
    b. a picnic
    c. a house and a family

21. In *I Got You (I Feel Good)*, when James Brown holds his girlfriend in his arms, what does he feel he can't do?

a. express how he feels
b. anything wrong
c. get any closer

22. According to Jackie Wilson in *Higher and Higher*, what was his closest friend prior to his uplifting experience with you?
    a. his music
    b. his car
    c. disappointment

23. When what thing happens do the Platters say *Smoke Gets in Your Eyes*?
    a. when cigarettes fill the air
    b. when a lovely flame dies
    c. when your woman falls for another man

24. In *Mama Said*, what was the name of the boy the Shirelles met?
    a. Jimmy
    b. Johnny
    c. Billy-Joe

25. In *Use Me Up*, what do Bill Withers's friends think it's their duty to tell him?
    a. that all his girlfriend wants to do is use him
    b. how to run his life
    c. how to spend all his money

26. Who told the Supremes *You Can't Hurry Love*?
    a. their boyfriend
    b. their mother
    c. their friends

27. Although in *The Tracks of My Tears* Smokey Robinson and the Miracles are laughing loud and hearty, how do they feel inside?
    a. calm and content
    b. jealous and angry
    c. blue

28. In *The Way You Do the Things You Do*, the Temptations claim that the way their girlfriend smells, she could have been ___.
    a. a six-course dinner
    b. perfume
    c. a summer's day

29. What do the Chiffons say you will be proud to have *One Fine Day*?
    a. them by your side
    b. a house in the country
    c. money in the bank

30. Why doesn't anyone want Jack to stay around in Ray Charles's *Hit the Road, Jack*?
    a. he's a wanted fugitive
    b. he's broke
    c. he never told anyone he was coming

31. In *Some Kind of Wonderful*, what does the Drifters' sweetheart do to show them that she understands?
    a. she nods her head
    b. she nibbles on their ear
    c. she touches their hand

32. Before Gene Chandler first met his girlfriend in *Groovy Situation*, how were both feeling?
    a. in love
    b. happy
    c. lonely

33. What did Boyz II Men do *In the Still of the Night*?
    a. they phoned you
    b. they left you behind
    c. they held you

34. James and Bobby Purify say in *I'm Your Puppet* that if you snap your fingers, they'll do what?
    a. give you whatever you want

    b. turn you some flips

    c. get pissed off at you

35. In *My World Is Empty Without You*, from what is there no hiding place for the Supremes?

    a. your face

    b. your bill collectors

    c. loneliness

36. In *Shotgun*, what do Jr. Walker and the All Stars say you should put on to do the jerk?

    a. high-heeled shoes

    b. pink shoelaces

    c. blue jeans

37. In *Ain't That Peculiar*, Marvin Gaye questions why his love is made stronger by ___.

    a. marriage

    b. lies

    c. suspicion

38. In *Remember (Walkin' in the Sand)*, what did the letter the Shangri-Las received say to them?

    a. their boyfriend had found somebody new

    b. they had won the million-dollar sweepstakes

    c. their lover had just been drafted

39. In *Then He Kissed Me*, what were the skies like when the Crystals were first kissed by their new beau?

    a. there was a full moon

    b. there was a total eclipse

    c. the stars were shining bright

40. If his best friend put a man's wife down, what does Percy Sledge say the man would do *When a Man Loves a Woman*?

    a. take his wife and the best friend to court

    b. leave

    c. turn his back on the best friend

41. Wherever their *Soldier Boy* goes, what do the Shirelles say will follow?

   a. their heart

   b. the memories of the girls he left at every port

   c. new families

42. In *Sunny,* what does Bobby Hebb say about how he felt yesterday?

   a. he didn't have a care in the world

   b. love was such an easy game to play

   c. his life was filled with rain

43. Although the Drifters say it's okay to dance with others in *Save the Last Dance for Me,* what do they remind you about after the evening is through?

   a. you've got their car keys

   b. don't go looking for them

   c. don't forget who's taking you home

44. In *Goin' Out of My Head,* why do Little Anthony and the Imperials feel an unrequited love each morning they see their lady-hopeful?

   a. she's already married

   b. they're too shy to say hello

   c. she just walks past them

45. When the Delfonics sing *La La Means I Love You,* what do they say they don't wear?

   a. a diamond ring

   b. fancy clothes

   c. underwear

46. In *The Tears of a Clown,* what do Smokey Robinson and the Miracles say is the reason they might be wearing a smile?

   a. to fool the public

   b. to show how much they love you

   c. it's what they get paid to be doing

47. What do the Penguins hope and pray in *Earth Angel?*
    a. one day they'll marry you and take you home
    b. they'll be the vision of your happiness
    c. you'll come and visit them in their dreams

48. In *What's Love Got to Do With It,* although the touch of your hand makes Tina Turner's pulse race, how does she explain the reason for the thrill?
    a. it's only because opposites attract
    b. it's only human nature
    c. she hasn't seen you for awhile, so it's only something new

49. According to Arthur Conley in *Sweet Soul Music,* who's the king of them all?
    a. James Brown
    b. Elvis Presley
    c. Mohammed Ali

50. How long do the Manhattans plan to stay by their *Shining Star?*
    a. until their dying day
    b. until her glow is gone
    c. until the sun no longer shines

QUIZ B

1. In *Back in My Arms Again,* why don't the Supremes listen to friends' advice?
   a. because their friends are secretly jealous and don't want them together
   b. they're so blindly in love, nothing can save them now
   c. because all advice ever got them was spending long and lonely nights

2. Why do the Chiffons caution others to stay away from the *Sweet Talkin' Guy* and not give him love?

   a. because he belongs to them
   b. because tomorrow he's on his way
   c. because in nine months you'll have a sweet-talking baby

3. In *My Girl*, what do the Temptations have on a cloudy day?

   a. rain
   b. an excuse to call you
   c. sunshine

4. Why does Aretha Franklin say in *Respect* that she isn't going to do her man any wrong?

   a. because she doesn't want to
   b. because she's done it before, and she won't do it anymore
   c. he's a fool who'll believe anything she promises

5. According to the Spinners in *Could It Be I'm Falling in Love*, who is responsible for specially making their girlfriend?

   a. her mother
   b. heaven
   c. an angel

6. When the Righteous Brothers kiss your lips, why do they now say *You've Lost That Loving Feeling*?

   a. your lips don't taste sweet anymore
   b. you don't let them do anything else
   c. you never close your eyes anymore

7. In *Keep the Ball Rolling*, what is the name of the game according to Jay and the Techniques?

   a. soccer
   b. love
   c. jacks

8. In *He's a Rebel*, how does the Crystals' boyfriend walk by?
   a. with a bad attitude
   b. proudly
   c. softly and quietly

9. In *For Once in My Life*, what had hurt Stevie Wonder in the past?
   a. low-flying Frisbees
   b. sorrow
   c. love

10. While *Standing in the Shadows of Love*, who is the Four Tops' only company?
    a. misery
    b. the lonely crowd
    c. one friend

11. In *Ain't Too Proud to Beg*, what have the Temptations heard about a crying man?
    a. he's a coward who has no beliefs
    b. he's a person who is loved and who cares
    c. he's half a man with no sense of pride

12. In *Another Saturday Night*, what does Sam Cooke say he'd be doing if he were home?
    a. waiting for your phone call
    b. watching *Leave It to Beaver*
    c. swinging with two chicks

13. For Marvin Gaye and Tammi Terrell, with every passing minute of *Your Precious Love*, what is wrapped up in their life?
    a. joy
    b. another minute wasted
    c. another memory

14. In *Band of Gold*, where does Freda Payne wait, hoping for her husband to return?

a. in the bathroom
b. in the lobby
c. in her room

15. On what corner in *Kansas City* will Wilbert Harrison be standing?
    a. 12th Street and Vine
    b. Beverly and Wilshire
    c. Haight and Ashbury

16. In *Please Mr. Postman*, what message are the Marvelettes hoping for?
    a. a card or letter saying their boyfriend is returning
    b. a telegram telling them they've won the talent contest
    c. a reply concerning their marriage plans

17. In *Land of a Thousand Dances*, Wilson Pickett asks us to do the Pony like ___.
    a. his girl Joanie
    b. Boney Maroney
    c. Sandy and Tony

18. What is Marvin Gaye referring to when he says *How Sweet It Is*?
    a. how it is to be loved by you
    b. how it tastes to have a peanut butter sandwich made by you
    c. his impersonation of Jackie Gleason

19. In *Knock on Wood*, how does Eddie Floyd describe his girlfriend's love?
    a. it's like thunder and lightning
    b. it's like sitting on a bed of nails
    c. it's the icing on his cake

20. According to Friends of Distinction, *Grazing in the Grass* is ___.
    a. a gas

    b. groovy

    c. a pain in the ass

21. Because of whom do Martha and the Vandellas feel as though they are stuck in *Quicksand?*

    a. their two boyfriends

    b. you

    c. their parents

22. Sam Cooke tells us that the people on the *Chain Gang* work all day until ___.

    a. the sun goes down

    b. the clock strikes five

    c. they feel like quitting

23. Why are Little Anthony and the Imperials *Goin' Out Of My Head?*

    a. they can't explain the tears they shed

    b. you just left them for another guy

    c. they feel so happy in love

24. According to Soul II Soul in *Keep On Movin',* what is yellow the color of?

    a. their love's hair

    b. the sun's rays

    c. city snow

25. When the Drifters are *Under the Boardwalk,* who is with them?

    a. the pigeons and the doves

    b. roaches and ants

    c. their baby

26. Why do the Manhattans have to *Kiss and Say Goodbye?*

    a. so they can see you again tomorrow

    b. because of their obligations

    c. because they've got more girls to meet

27. According to the Isley Brothers, *It's Your Thing* to do what?

    a. have three boyfriends
    b. go skinny-dipping
    c. whatever you want to do

28. In *Where Did Our Love Go*, with what do the Supremes compare the intensity of the burning love they had experienced?
    a. a bee sting
    b. the sun
    c. an oven

29. In *Hurts So Bad*, what do Little Anthony and the Imperials say you don't know?
    a. how to make them feel good
    b. how to dance
    c. what they're going through

30. In *Uptight (Everything's Alright)*, Stevie Wonder knows that he's just an ___.
    a. entertainer
    b. idle dreamer
    c. average guy

31. In *Everyday People*, Sly and the Family Stone are confused that though you love and hate and know them, you still can't figure out ___.
    a. who you are
    b. why you'd never want them to move into your neighborhood
    c. the bag they're in

32. In *It's the Same Old Song*, what one thing did the Four Tops enjoy doing when the music was playing?
    a. making romance
    b. conversing
    c. cooking

33. The Marvelettes tell their *Playboy* acquaintance that he'd better find himself another ___.

a. bunny
b. toy
c. playgirl

34. According to Martha and the Vandellas, what season is perfect for *Dancing in the Street?*

a. spring
b. summer
c. winter

35. As long as Ben E. King knows you'll *Stand by Me*, when the night has come he won't be ___.

a. afraid
b. leaving
c. crying

36. In *He's So Fine*, what kind of hair does the Chiffons' dreamboat have?

a. wavy
b. curly
c. velvety

37. According to the Main Ingredient, *Everybody Plays the Fool Sometimes* because, although you may love someone else, there's no guarantee that ___.

a. they're worth loving
b. they won't leech off you
c. they're going to love you

38. Where did the Shangri-Las meet the *Leader of the Pack?*

a. at the drive-in
b. at the cemetery
c. at the candy store

39. In *Boys*, what have the Shirelles been told happens when a boy kisses a girl?

a. he takes a trip around the world
b. he's in love to stay
c. a star falls from the sky

40. Marvin Gaye jubilantly says to Tammi Terrell that there *Ain't No Mountain High Enough* to keep him from ___.
    a. leaving her
    b. climbing into her heart
    c. getting to her

41. Why was Bobby Lewis *Tossin' and Turnin'* last night, unable to sleep?
    a. he had a Mexican dinner
    b. he was thinking of you
    c. his mother-in-law moved in

42. Where are Dee Clark's *Raindrops* falling from?
    a. the clouds above
    b. his nose
    c. his eyes

43. What are the names of the two guys the Marvelettes recommend selecting from so that you *Don't Mess With Bill*?
    a. Tommy and Bobby
    b. Frank and Jim
    c. Ringo and Phil

44. In *Papa's Got a Brand New Bag*, James Brown says that papa isn't a ___.
    a. dope
    b. drag
    c. dinosaur

45. What comes tumbling down for Wilson Pickett *In the Midnight Hour*?
    a. his tears
    b. his roof
    c. his love

46. In *Get Ready*, what do the Temptations reply when asked who it is that makes their dreams real?
    a. any girl who says hello

   b. why ask such a stupid question?

   c. you do

47. What do Jay and the Techniques plan to do shortly to make sure their *Apples, Peaches, Pumpkin Pie* sweetheart doesn't roam from them?

   a. move in with her

   b. lock her up

   c. marry her

48. After finding that Aretha Franklin is just a link in the *Chain of Fools*, what does her father tell her to do?

   a. come home

   b. break the chain

   c. take it in stride

49. According to Fats Domino, what melody does the wind in the willow play atop *Blueberry Hill*?

   a. a melody of magic

   b. love's sweet melody

   c. a blend of the blues

50. In *What Does It Take (to Win Your Love for Me)*, what are Junior Walker and the All-Stars trying to show you?

   a. how much they love you

   b. how well they can dance

   c. that you don't need anybody else

BONUS QUIZ

  1. Joe Jones says *You Talk Too Much* to the point that you even worry his ____.

   a. ulcer

   b. folks

   c. pet

  2. Why do Cornelius Brothers and Sister Rose say *It's Too Late to Turn Back Now*?

    a. they've been caught telling too many lies

    b. you've left them for another man

    c. they believe they're falling in love

3. When is it the Supremes say *I Hear a Symphony?*

    a. all through the day

    b. whenever you're near

    c. whenever they turn on their favorite oldies station

4. According to Tone Loc in *Wild Thing*, what was he doing all week?

    a. thinking of you

    b. working

    c. watching you dance

5. In *Don't Play That Song*, what does Ben E. King say the song fills his heart with?

    a. pain

    b. memories

    c. hope

6. In *Why Do Fools Fall in Love*, who do Frankie Lymon and the Teenagers say await the break of day?

    a. lovers

    b. birds

    c. fools

7. By what time is Lee Dorsey already up and *Working in the Coal Mine?*

    a. 6:30 A.M.

    b. noon

    c. 5:00 A.M.

8. In *Will You Love Me Tomorrow*, the Shirelles want to know if their relationship will be a lasting treasure or whether it's only a ___.

    a. one-night's leisure

    b. moment's pleasure

    c. trophy for you to measure

9. In *Unchained Melody,* how does time pass for the Righteous Brothers?
   a. without meaning
   b. too fast
   c. so slowly

10. When Soul II Soul are coming *Back to Life*, where are they returning from?
    a. a nightmare
    b. a fantasy
    c. a life of loneliness

11. When taking the *Midnight Train to Georgia*, where was Gladys Knight and the Pips' boyfriend coming from?
    a. Dallas
    b. New York
    c. Los Angeles

12. As your *Soul Man*, Sam and Dave will give you hope and be your only ___.
    a. boyfriend
    b. lover
    c. soul mate

13. In *Ready for Love*, how do Martha and the Vandellas feel for the first time in their lives?
    a. content
    b. alone
    c. lucky

14. According to Naughty by Nature, what do the letters of O.P.P. most closely stand for?
    a. other people's property
    b. OK to party, party
    c. October's prom plans

15. Although you may never become a rich man at the *Car Wash*, what does Rose Royce say it's better than doing?

    a. being a bum
    b. shining shoes
    c. digging a ditch

16. According to the Platters, when is a person *Enchanted*?
    a. when he touches a star
    b. when a lover calls
    c. after a good meal

17. With whom does Lloyd Price's *Stagger Lee* get in a quarrel?
    a. Slim
    b. his wife
    c. Billy

18. In *Parents Just Don't Understand*, where did D.J. Jazzy Jeff and the Fresh Prince stop with the foxy chick they picked up?
    a. at McDonald's
    b. at a local bar
    c. at her house

19. What do the Coasters have to do in *Yakety Yak* if they want some spending money?
    a. get off the telephone
    b. take out the papers and the trash
    c. get a job

20. According to Young M.C. in *Bust a Move*, what happens when guys play hard to get?
    a. the women get jealous
    b. they don't get anything
    c. they make the girls go crazy

American Rock:
The First Two Decades
(1950s-1960s)

From the early sounds of Dion to the later blends of
the Four Seasons, America has always had a love
affair with vocal harmony set to a dance beat. Solo
greats such as Del Shannon, Lou Christie, and Dusty
Springfield, and groups such as the Beach Boys, Paul
Revere and the Raiders, and the Grass Roots kept the
groove going throughout the 1960s, And when these
grooves were coupled with the haunting lyrics of
Bob Dylan and the equal-rights pleas of Lesley Gore,
the results were destined to shape future genera-
tions of rockers. The words and beat of the earliest
American rockers are alive and well today, in the
repertoire of America's top rock bands.

QUIZ A

1. In *Green River*, who is calling to Creedence Clearwater Revival?
   a. their mother
   b. a barefoot girl
   c. bullfrogs

2. Del Shannon wants his *Runaway* to return home to end his ___.

   a. life
   b. misery
   c. loneliness

3. In *Rain on the Roof,* what is the Lovin' Spoonful caught up in?

   a. a summer shower
   b. lies
   c. love

4. In *Dirty Water,* what city do the Standells call home?

   a. San Francisco
   b. Chicago
   c. Boston

5. What two kinds of cars does the Rip Chords' *Little Cobra* race against?

   a. Mustangs and Corvettes
   b. Stingrays and Jaguars
   c. Toyotas and VW's

6. Barry McGuire feels that we're on the *Eve of Destruction* because what is disintegrating?

   a. human respect
   b. the ozone layer
   c. common sense

7. Although the Spiral Staircase says they'll love you *More Today Than Yesterday,* how does this amount compare to how much they'll love you tomorrow?

   a. only half as much as tomorrow
   b. only time will tell
   c. it won't compare

8. For Jay and the Americans, *This Magic Moment* is sweeter than wine and softer than ___.

   a. a summer's night

    b. a pillow

    c. a box of tissue

9. The Byrds want *Mr. Tambourine Man* to take them on a journey aboard what kind of vehicle?

    a. a tambourine

    b. a ship

    c. a magic carpet

10. In *Never My Love*, what does the Association say you are afraid they might one day do?

    a. cheat on you

    b. change their mind

    c. go all the way

11. In *Spinning Wheel*, where do Blood, Sweat and Tears suggest you drop all your troubles?

    a. in the garbage dump

    b. by the riverside

    c. in their lap

12. What do the odds suggest for Johnny Rivers's *Secret Agent Man?*

    a. his identity will be discovered

    b. Uncle Sam won't know where to send his next paycheck

    c. he won't live to see tomorrow

13. Although ? (Question Mark) and the Mysterians want to levy equal justice against their ex-girlfriend, what does ? feel he has too many of to carry on?

    a. heartaches

    b. questions

    c. teardrops

14. How much did Ronny and the Daytonas pay for their *Bucket "T"?*

    a. $500

    b. $5

    c. $5000

15. John Fred and His Playboy Band's *Judy in Disguise (With Glasses)* has ___ eyes.
    a. cantaloupe
    b. blood-shot
    c. marshmallow

16. When Randy and the Rainbows walk with *Denise*, what does it feel like?
    a. floating on air
    b. a drag
    c. paradise

17. On what day are the Young Rascals *Groovin'*?
    a. every day
    b. Sunday
    c. Saturday

18. After six hours of school, what do the Beach Boys do right away in *Dance, Dance, Dance*?
    a. change clothes and head for the beach
    b. check the newspapers for the next dance
    c. turn the radio volume up

19. *Candy Girl* sets the Four Seasons' hearts awhirl with what three things?
    a. her walkin', talkin', and affection
    b. her clothes, boyfriends, and sweet kisses
    c. her huggin', kissin', and lovin'

20. According to the Doors in *Riders on the Storm*, who is waiting on the road?
    a. a killer
    b. your neighbor
    c. they are

21. In *You Didn't Have to Be So Nice*, what did today indicate for the Lovin' Spoonful?
    a. they should have called her yesterday

   b. the time was right to follow her

   c. they had to treat her right or say goodnight

22. In *The 59th Street Bridge Song (Feelin' Groovy)*, why does Harpers Bizarre advise that you should slow down?

   a. you've got to make the morning last

   b. you're going to get a heart attack

   c. there's a cop giving tickets

23. In *In-A-Gadda-Da-Vida*, what does the Iron Butterfly want you to do with them?

   a. raise a family

   b. walk upon the land

   c. learn English

24. In *Judy's Turn to Cry,* what is the name of Lesley Gore's boyfriend?

   a. Johnny

   b. Bobby

   c. Tommy

25. In *Bread and Butter,* what do the Newbeats see their baby eating with another man?

   a. a Big Mac

   b. chicken and dumplings

   c. peanut butter

26. According to Dusty Springfield in *You Don't Have to Say You Love Me*, her boyfriend doesn't need to stay at home but simply ___.

   a. call every hour

   b. be close at hand

   c. think of her every night

27. What does the Ad Libs' *Boy From New York City* have that is the finest in town?

   a. a penthouse

   b. a Lamborghini

   c. groupies

28. In *Like a Rolling Stone*, Bob Dylan says that when you don't have anything, ___.
    a. there's only one way up
    b. everything looks good
    c. you've got nothing to lose

29. In *Dedicated to the One I Love*, what do The Mamas and the Papas need you to do for them while they are far away?
    a. feed the cat
    b. pray
    c. leave on your love light

30. When Lou Christie settles down in *Lightnin' Strikes*, what does he want on his mind?
    a. all the girls he's loved before
    b. the way to find happiness
    c. one woman

31. Where are the Beach Boys' Good *Vibrations* coming from?
    a. surfing
    b. love
    c. nervousness

32. In *Along Comes Mary*, the Association's empty cup tastes as sweet as ___.
    a. punch
    b. honey
    c. her lips

33. The Strawberry Alarm Clock claims in *Incense and Peppermints* that there is little to win and ___.
    a. no time to try
    b. nothing to lose
    c. so much to lose

34. In *Big Girls Don't Cry*, what happened that showed the Four Seasons that big girls do cry?

a. you cried when they broke your Beatles albums
b. your mama said you cried in bed
c. they saw you cry tears of joy

35. In *San Francisco (Wear Some Flowers in Your Hair),* what kind of people does Scott McKenzie say you'll meet there?
   a. gentle
   b. gay
   c. wild and crazy

36. The Lovin' Spoonful is lost in a *Daydream* about what?
   a. their bundle of joy
   b. a delicious barbecue steak dinner
   c. Friday night

37. In *Hungry,* what is this need doing to Paul Revere and the Raiders?
   a. it's making them homeless
   b. it's driving them insane
   c. it's turning them into junkies

38. In *Time Won't Let Me,* what have the Outsiders waited too long for?
   a. a chance to hold you in their arms
   b. their weekly paycheck
   c. for you to say goodbye to your other boyfriend

39. Although the Casinos say in *Then You Can Tell Me Goodbye* that they won't grieve if you go, how long do they first want you to wait?
   a. a lifetime
   b. until they finish eating
   c. a year

40. At what hour are the Soul Survivors caught in the traffic jam on the *Expressway to Your Heart?*
   a. 8:00 A.M.

    b. noon

    c. 5:00 P.M.

41. In *Lady Willpower*, what do Gary Puckett and the Union Gap tell their girlfriend that it's now or never to do?

    a. get married

    b. give her love to them

    c. get an abortion

42. In *Sealed With a Kiss*, for what duration of time will Brian Hyland not be seeing you?

    a. until he returns from Vietnam

    b. for a week

    c. for the summer

43. In *Easier Said Than Done*, even though the members of the Essex love a boy so much, why are they afraid he'll never know of their love for him?

    a. they don't speak Spanish

    b. they get so timid and shy

    c. he's moving away

44. In *Traces*, what word do the Classics IV use to describe their old photographs?

    a. faded

    b. magical

    c. valuable

45. According to the Buckinghams in *Mercy, Mercy, Mercy*, what will everybody in the neighborhood testify to?

    a. her infidelity

    b. her religious enthusiasm

    c. her good looks

46. What did Gary Lewis and the Playboys' girlfriend do that indicates *This Diamond Ring* no longer means anything?

    a. she cheated on them

    b. she took it off her finger
    c. she pawned it

47. The Music Explosion feels that with *A Little Bit of Soul* you can go through life and more easily ___.
    a. avoid fights
    b. make lasting friends
    c. reach your goal

48. In Lesley Gore's *It's My Party,* which two people left unexpectedly together?
    a. Johnny and Judy
    b. Jimmy and Joanie
    c. Tommy and Billy

49. In *I Think We're Alone Now,* what do the older people tell Tommy James and the Shondells when they are together with you?
    a. if they do anything, don't get caught
    b. treat you with respect
    c. behave

50. The Grass Roots say *Let's Live for Today* while everyone else is chasing after what?
    a. tomorrow
    b. dreams that can't come true
    c. the other guy's wife

QUIZ B

1. In *She'd Rather Be With Me,* what one word describes the kind of guys the Turtles say they are to have such a girl?
    a. fools
    b. blessed
    c. lucky

2. In *Come a Little Bit Closer,* where are Jay and the Americans to be found?

   a. in a café
   b. in a movie theater
   c. on the beach

3. In *Five O'Clock World*, what is pounding through the Vogues' brains?

   a. suspicions
   b. the sounds of the city
   c. the ticking of the clock

4. Who else in their family went with the Beach Boys aboard the *Sloop John B?*

   a. their father
   b. their girlfriend
   c. their grandfather

5. When we look over yonder in *Crystal Blue Persuasion*, what do Tommy James and the Shondells say we'll see rising?

   a. the stock market
   b. two lovers in the dawn
   c. the sun

6. What do the Byrds want *Mr. Spaceman* to do for them?

   a. introduce them to his daughter
   b. give them some drugs
   c. take them for a ride

7. In *Last Kiss*, who took J. Frank Wilson's girlfriend away from him?

   a. the Lord
   b. another guy
   c. her parents

8. What one thing do the Exciters say you must *Tell Him* if you really love him?

   a. how big and strong he is
   b. that you'll never leave him
   c. that nothing else matters to you

9. What do the Classics IV ask their *Spooky* girlfriend in the evening when everything is getting groovy?
   a. if it's true she's really just a floozie
   b. if she'd like to go with them and hootchie kootchie
   c. if she wants to go to see a movie

10. In *I've Been Lonely Too Long*, what do the Young Rascals feel they can't go on anymore without?
    a. love
    b. friends
    c. dreams

11. What do the Hondells want you to wear when they go riding with you on their *Little Honda*?
    a. a ragged sweatshirt
    b. jeans and a terry top
    c. a two-piece bikini

12. Paul Anka wants you to *Put Your Head on My Shoulder* and show him ___.
    a. that you love him
    b. your high school yearbook
    c. what's on your mind

13. What does Jimmy Jones say *Good Timin'* did for him?
    a. it made him rich
    b. it brought him to you
    c. it told him when to stop foolin' around

14. In *Did You Ever Have to Make Up Your Mind*, the Lovin' Spoonful cautions that the decision is not always easy or ___.
    a. fair
    b. kind
    c. permanent

15. According to Billy Joe Royal in *Cherry Hill Park*, what did Mary Hill go away one day to do?

    a. get married
    b. become a Peace Corps volunteer
    c. drive a truck

16. What do Gary Puckett and the Union Gap accusingly ask their *Woman, Woman*?
    a. Did you see my wallet around?
    b. Have you got cheating on your mind?
    c. Where were you when I called last night?

17. Although *Johnny Angel* is an angel to Shelley Fabares, what is the problem with their relationship?
    a. he's scatterbrained and wimpy
    b. he doesn't know that she exists
    c. he's already going steady with another girl

18. Norman Greenbaum feels that in order to go to the *Spirit in the Sky* one day, whom must you have a friend in?
    a. your lover
    b. Jesus
    c. everyone

19. In *Don't Worry Baby*, the Beach Boys feel they should have kept their mouth shut when they started to brag about what?
    a. their girlfriend
    b. their school grades
    c. their car

20. In *Rhythm of the Rain*, what has happened to the only girl the Cascades care about?
    a. she's getting married
    b. she's gone away
    c. she's gotten hooked on drugs

21. According to Bob Dylan in *Positively 4th Street*, what did you do when he was down?

   a. you helped him up
   b. you stood there, grinning
   c. you knelt down beside him

22. In *We Ain't Got Nothin' Yet*, the Blues Magoos caution that you can't face the world with your head ____.
   a. between your legs
   b. to the ground
   c. all awhirl

23. In *I Had Too Much to Dream*, the Electric Prunes touched their dream girl's golden hair and tasted her ____.
   a. perfume
   b. sweet lips
   c. luscious legs

24. When Steppenwolf says for you to close your eyes in *Magic Carpet Ride*, what will then take you away?
   a. the magic carpet
   b. the sounds
   c. fantasy

25. What name does Dion, *The Wanderer*, have tattooed on his chest?
   a. Dion
   b. Ruby
   c. Rosie

26. In *For What It's Worth*, the Buffalo Springfield informs us there's a man over there telling them that they've got to ____.
   a. cut their hair
   b. leave
   c. beware

27. In *Light My Fire*, the Doors claim they'd be a liar if they were to say ____.

    a. they don't love you with desire
    b. they couldn't get much higher
    c. they can't even change a tire

28. In *Take Good Care of My Baby*, why are tears falling for Bobby Vee?
    a. another boy has taken you from him
    b. he's lonely and blue
    c. he knows you've been untrue

29. In order to be rolling on the river with *Proud Mary*, Creedence Clearwater Revival left a job in ___.
    a. the coal mine
    b. Memphis
    c. the city

30. In *Suite: Judy Blue Eyes*, Crosby, Stills and Nash say it's getting to the point where they are ___.
    a. confused
    b. ready to go all the way
    c. no fun anymore

31. In *Do You Believe In Magic?* the Lovin' Spoonful says that music in a young girl's heart can free her whenever ___.
    a. it starts
    b. hangups leave her
    c. they see her

32. The Syndicate of Sound tells their *Little Girl* that she hadn't done anything to them that ___.
    a. was immoral
    b. could ever leave a scar
    c. hadn't been done before

33. How much did each word of the *Western Union* telegram cost the Five Americans?
    a. fifteen cents

    b. a quarter

    c. sixty cents

34. In *Johnny Get Angry*, what does Joanie Sommers want her boyfriend to give her, to show her that he is a caveman and the boss?

    a. a lecture

    b. a kiss

    c. a stiff one

35. If their girlfriend wants to make Dion and the Belmonts cry in *A Teenager in Love*, how difficult will it be?

    a. not so hard

    c. impossible

    c. easy if she hits them in the right place

36. According to Bob Kuban and the In-Men, what will *The Cheater* do once he takes your girl?

    a. he'll laugh at you

    b. he'll love her madly

    c. he'll mistreat her

37. Because the *Image of a Girl* was on their mind and they couldn't sleep, what did the Safaris hear while lying on their bed?

    a. the milkman

    b. the clock

    c. her voice

38. In *Hushabye*, what do the Mystics call to the guardian angels up above to do?

    a. give them an angel to love

    b. quit bothering them with thoughts of love

    c. take care of the one they love

39. What do the Four Seasons advise *Dawn* to think about before she decides to go out with them?

    a. if they can really provide a happy home for her

    b. what the future would be if she stayed with them

    c. where they are going to spend the night

40. What kind of establishment is the wooden building Jimmy Gilmer and the Fireballs nicknamed the *Sugar Shack?*

    a. a bar

    b. a coffeehouse

    c. a bowling alley

41. In *All Along the Watchtower,* how many riders does Jimi Hendrix say were approaching as the wind began to howl?

    a. two

    b. several

    c. ten

42. Besides saying *I'd Wait a Million Years,* what do the Grass Roots say they would expend a million of?

    a. wishes and fears

    b. prayers

    c. tears

43. According to Jan and Dean, what is the ratio of females to males in *Surf City?*

    a. five to one

    b. there are no girls in Surf City

    c. two to one

44. When the Sensations wanted somebody to *Let Me In,* what did they think before but later were not too sure of?

    a. that you were their friend

    b. whether you were really in there

    c. that they were on the right block

45. For how long does Johnny Burnette plan to keep *Dreamin'?*

    a. until the morning comes
    b. forever
    c. until his dreaming comes true

46. Bobby Vee is treated so carelessly in *Rubber Ball* that when he's with his girlfriend, what does she call him?
    a. by some other boy's name
    b. John
    c. Number Six

47. In *Hats Off to Larry,* what does Del Shannon say it's your turn to do now that Larry said goodbye?
    a. leave
    b. cry
    c. start living with your mother

48. *Although Only Love Can Break a Heart,* what does Gene Pitney add is also true?
    a. only love can mend it again
    b. you can't break a heart you never had
    c. true love is everlasting

49. In *Save Your Heart for Me,* what do Gary Lewis and the Playboys say someone's going to do when you are all alone, far away from home?
    a. tempt them
    b. flirt with you
    c. rob your house

50. In *Cara Mia,* what do Jay and the Americans question?
    a. why you are so lovely
    b. why they must say goodbye
    c. if you can understand how they feel

BONUS QUIZ

1. According to the Doors, what does the *Wishful Sinful* crystal water cover everything in?
   a. blue
   b. shades of grey
   c. swirling greens and oranges

2. According to Peter, Paul, and Mary, who was *Stewball*?
   a. the town drunk
   b. a wandering minstrel
   c. a racehorse

3. What do Ronny and the Daytonas ask *Sandy* whether she can remember?
   a. when they first met
   b. when they were her chosen one
   c. their first day of school together

4. What two people did the Regents dance with before realizing that only *Barbara Ann* would do?
   a. Bony Maroney and Little Miss Lucy
   b. Betty Lou and Peggy Sue
   c. Sally and Janie

5. During that *Wonderful Summer*, where did Robin Ward stroll with you?
   a. along the sand
   b. down Sunset Strip
   c. through Central Park

6. According to the Orlons, *South Street* is where which group of people meets?
   a. the in-crowd
   b. all the groovy cats
   c. the hippies

7. According to the Kingsmen, why wasn't the girlfriend of the *Jolly Green Giant* aware of his unusual color?
   a. she was too much in love
   b. she was colorblind
   c. she never saw him during the day

8. In *1984*, why does Spirit claim that Big Brother is really not your friend?
   a. you won't need any friends then
   b. he's telling lies behind your back
   c. you're never out of his sight

9. What do Del Shannon and his girlfriend *Keep Searchin'* for?
   a. a love that cannot die
   b. the right words to say
   c. a place to hide

10. According to Ray Peterson in *Tell Laura I Love Her,* what was the name of Laura's boyfriend?
    a. Billy
    b. Tommy
    c. Johnny

11. In *Steppin' Out,* a situation involving who forced Paul Revere and the Raiders to leave town?
    a. the U.S. Army
    b. the Colombian drug cartel
    c. a record agent

12. In *She's About a Mover,* what question did the girl ask the Sir Douglas Quintet when she strolled up to them?
    a. what their name was
    b. whether they'd like to dance
    c. whether they were all alone

13. According to Gene Pitney in *The Man Who Shot Liberty Valance*, what was the only law that Liberty Valance understood?
    a. the point of a gun
    b. his law
    c. the law of love

14. In *Nobody But Me*, what two dances do the Human Beinz say they can't be beat in?
    a. twist and frug
    b. Bristol stomp and locomotion
    c. shingaling and bugaloo

15. In *You're the One*, although the Vogues admit there may be some tears through the coming years, what do they say will guide them through every mile?
    a. their faith in you
    b. your love
    c. the weekend

16. In *Drag City*, what kind of wheels does Jan and Dean's car have?
    a. chrome-reversed
    b. round
    c. positraction

17. In *Surfin'*, what do the Beach Boys do when the surf is down?
    a. walk with you on the sand
    b. dance to the Surfer Stomp
    c. pray for surf

18. In *Summer Means Fun*, where do the Rip Chords go surfing every day under the sun?
    a. Waikiki
    b. Santa Cruz
    c. Malibu

19. What is Johnny Crawford going to write for *Cindy's Birthday?*
    a. a love letter
    b. a symphony
    c. a birthday card

20. In *Love Her Madly,* how many horses do the Doors tell us are on the march?
    a. thirteen
    b. three
    c. seven

The British Invasion
(1964-1969)

Rock and roll was a purely American phenomenon until 1964, when the British Invasion took place. The Beatles led the charge, but they weren't alone. Rock and roll saw the likes of the long-haired Rolling Stones and Animals, together with more mild-mannered groups like Herman's Hermits and Gerry and the Pacemakers. These "invaders" set the world of rock and roll spinning in a new direction, solidifying its immortality on a global scale.

QUIZ A

1. In *Listen, People,* what do Herman's Hermits say they hope will never happen when you fall in love with someone?
   a. you'll part
   b. you'll take it too seriously
   c. it'll affect your freedom

2. According to Wayne Fontana and the Mindbenders in *The Game of Love,* what is the purpose for a man and a woman?
   a. to raise a family
   b. to break up and make up
   c. to love each other

3. On a *Carousel,* how do the Hollies get closer to their ladyfriend?
   a. by changing horses
   b. by sending letters
   c. by telling her friends that they really care

4. In *I Know a Place,* how does Petula Clark describe the lighting of this hideaway?
   a. psychedelic
   b. senuous and inviting
   c. always low

5. What do the Troggs want *With a Girl Like You?*
   a. to spend their life with you
   b. to take you everywhere they go
   c. to have you under their skin

6. What is the profession of the Rolling Stones' *Honky Tonk Woman?*
   a. rock musician
   b. barroom queen
   c. cab driver

7. For what do the Bee Gees have only *Words* on their side to do?
   a. take your heart away
   b. show their love is true
   c. defend themselves against the rumors

8. In what city is the Animals' *House of the Rising Sun* located?
   a. New Orleans
   b. Manchester
   c. Abilene

9. What is it that Freddie and the Dreamers say *I'm Telling You Now?*
   a. they don't want to see you again

    b. it's time to see the preacher
    c. they're in love with you

10. When Manfred Mann knew he was falling in love in *Do Wah Diddy Diddy,* what did he tell his girlfriend?
    a. about his wife and kids
    b. how the world was headed for destruction
    c. the things he'd been dreaming of

11. With what two senses does the Who's *Pinball Wizard* play the games?
    a. touch and hearing
    b. sight and taste
    c. intuition and smell

12. According to Herman's Hermits in *Wonderful World,* what one course don't they know much about?
    a. psychology
    b. botany
    c. geometry

13. In *Heart Full of Soul,* what question do the Yardbirds echo?
    a. Does anybody really know what time it is?
    b. Where is she?
    c. What is the reason for falling in love?

14. In *Love Potion Number Nine,* where did the Searchers' specialized chemist reside?
    a. on the corner of 34th and Vine
    b. on Haight and Ashbury Streets
    c. on the south side of Chicago

15. Although the Rolling Stones say you're searching for a good time, why do they add that *Time Is on My Side?*
    a. they know all your friends
    b. you'll come running back to them
    c. you've got no place else to go

16. In *A Groovy Kind of Love*, when the Mindbenders are feeling blue, what do they do to remedy the feeling?
    a. take a look at you
    b. take an Alka Seltzer
    c. put on your favorite radio station

17. According to Gerry and the Pacemakers in *Don't Let the Sun Catch You Crying*, when is the right time to cry?
    a. anytime you want to
    b. no time
    c. the nighttime

18. According to the Walker Brothers in *Make It Easy on Yourself*, what is so very hard to do?
    a. break up
    b. find that special angel
    c. remain faithful

19. In *We Gotta Get Out of This Place*, what words of despair do the Animals' friends tell them?
    a. there ain't no use in tryin'
    b. you're stuck here forever
    c. nobody buys your records anymore

20. In *There Is a Mountain*, what does Donovan see upon his garden?
    a. weeds
    b. a daffodil
    c. a snail

21. In *Can't You Hear My Heart Beat*, what is the explanation Herman's Hermits give for their unusual palpitations?
    a. you're the one they love
    b. the food's giving them gas
    c. you're the doctor and you've got the cure

22. In what parts of their body do the Troggs feel that *Love Is All Around?*
    a. heart and tummy
    b. fingers and toes
    c. nose and ears

23. In *Tuesday Afternoon,* what is drawing the Moody Blues near?
    a. your words of love
    b. the sounds of silence
    c. the trees

24. Although *Silence Is Golden,* what can't the Tremeloes ignore?
    a. that their eyes still see
    b. the writing on the wall
    c. their mother-in-law

25. In *To Love Somebody,* what do the Bee Gees say everybody has been telling them?
    a. everybody's somebody's fool
    b. there's a way to do every little thing
    c. everybody loves somebody sometime

26. While watching television, what does a man tell the Rolling Stones that helps reinforce the idea that *(I Can't Get No) Satisfaction?*
    a. how clean their breath should be
    b. that they need to take singing lessons
    c. how white their shirts should be

27. What are the Kinks doing on a *Sunny Afternoon?*
    a. being lazy
    b. working
    c. making love

28. The Foundations are dismayed because they feel their girlfriend simply wants to *Build Me Up, Buttercup* to then do what?

a. rip them off
b. let them down
c. shatter their pride

29. In *How Do You Do It*, what would Gerry and the Pacemakers do if they knew how you do it to them?
a. they'd bottle the stuff
b. they'd take you to court
c. they'd do it to you

30. In *Don't Let Me Be Misunderstood*, the Animals claim that they're just a soul ___.
a. without a heart
b. whose intentions are good
c. trying to be free

31. In *Walk Away Renee*, what do the empty sidewalks cry out to the Left Banke?
a. don't tread on me
b. you're not to blame
c. that's the way love is

32. What is it that Herman's Hermits are grateful *Dandy* will always be?
a. a friend to them
b. happy
c. a bachelor

33. Why do the Zombies advise the other boy to *Tell Her No* even if she tempts him with her charms?
a. she's a tease
b. her love belongs to them
c. then he'll have her under his thumb

34. Crispian St. Peters says that he's *The Pied Piper*, and if you follow him he'll ___.
a. show you where it's at
b. play you a song
c. mess you up

35. Why do the Searchers have to hide their tears in *Needles and Pins?*

    a. crying is a sign of weakness
    b. other people are trying to steal them
    c. because of their pride

36. According to the Walker Brothers, *The Sun Ain't Gonna Shine Anymore* under what condition?

    a. when it's forever cloudy
    b. if we don't clean up the environment
    c. when you're without love

37. At what time did We Five discover *You Were on My Mind?*

    a. when they woke up this morning
    b. at the same time they discovered their car was missing
    c. last night, after dinner

38. What do the Seekers say nobody else could see inside *Georgie Girl?*

    a. her wild fantasies
    b. her loneliness
    c. a little girl hiding

39. According to Herman's Hermits, where is it that *There's a Kind of Hush?*

    a. wherever rumors exist
    b. all over the world
    c. in the library

40. In *Under My Thumb*, the Rolling Stones call their girlfriend what kind of pet?

    a. a teddy bear
    b. a hound dog
    c. a Siamese cat

41. Although the Fortunes claim *You've Got Your Troubles, I've Got Mine*, they nevertheless realize that

their friend has a worried look because his mate has ___.
a. left with the kids
b. found somebody to take his place
c. gone back home to her parents

42. In *Because*, what one thing do the Dave Clark Five want in order to be happy?
a. your hand
b. a magic genie
c. a kiss

43. What happened one day to the Bee Gees to cause all the lights to go out for them in *Massachusetts*?
a. they got hit by a bus
b. they left their girlfriend standing on her own
c. they forgot to pay their electric bill

44. When the Hollies were in school with *Carrie Ann*, what word describes the kinds of games they first played?
a. stupid
b. exciting
c. simple

45. In *Downtown*, Petula Clark says you'll soon be dancing to the gentle beat of which dance?
a. the bossa nova
b. the twist
c. the can-can

46. In *She's Not There*, although everyone else knew the truth about her, who told it to the Zombies?
a. their best friend
b. their mother
c. no one

47. In *You Really Got Me*, the Kinks always want to be ___.

a. bachelors
b. by your side
c. in love

48. What does Manfred Mann say everybody's feel-ing—especially every girl and boy—before *The Mighty Quinn* makes his appearance?
    a. despair
    b. excitement
    c. each other

49. In *A Whiter Shade of Pale*, how were Procol Harum feeling as the crowd called out for more drinks?
    a. drunk
    b. seasick
    c. thirsty

50. In *Get Off My Cloud*, what floor do the Rolling Stones have an apartment on?
    a. first
    b. thirteenth
    c. ninety-ninth

QUIZ B

1. Although the Kinks are *Tired of Waiting for You*, what do they nevertheless say about the way you spend your life?
   a. you know how to make the moments count
   b. you can do what you want
   c. if you're late, it's still better than being gone

2. According to Donovan in *Colours*, when is the time he loves the best?
   a. the morning
   b. sunset
   c. high noon

3. When did Herman's Hermits meet a new girl in the neighborhood which has made them feel *I'm Into Something Good?*
   a. today
   b. last night
   c. last week

4. In *Don't Sleep in the Subway,* why did Petula Clark's man walk out on her?
   a. he felt guilty for losing his job
   b. she said something stupid
   c. they both disagreed

5. What did the Dave Clark Five say *Over and Over* at the dance?
   a. I know she's here
   b. I can do it
   c. it's gonna be a drag

6. When was the Rolling Stones' *Jumpin' Jack Flash* born?
   a. on the Fourth of July
   b. during a hurricane
   c. as the clock struck midnight

7. What does *Wild Thing* do for the Troggs?
   a. she makes their heart sing
   b. she drives their thing wild
   c. she feeds them chicken and dumplings

8. In *Ferry Across the Mersey,* what do Gerry and the Pacemakers say people rush around everywhere with?
   a. their own secret cares
   b. secret lovers
   c. dreams that can't come true

9. For all that the Yardbirds would give *For Your Love,* what do they want you to specifically do at night?

    a. call them
    b. come by
    c. dream of them

10. What do the Hollies share with their friend in *Bus Stop?*
    a. a candy bar
    b. an umbrella
    c. their lifetime experiences

11. In *All Day and All of the Night,* the Kinks are not content to be with you ___.
    a. in the daytime
    b. with your mother around
    c. anymore

12. According to Cream in *Sunshine of Your Love,* the darkness approaches as lights close ___.
    a. the tired eyes
    b. in on lovers
    c. the icy streets

13. Talking about their *Brown Sugar,* around what time do the Rolling Stones say you should have heard her?
    a. midnight
    b. noon
    c. dawn

14. In *I Go to Pieces,* what do Peter and Gordon tell their eyes to do whey they see their ex-girlfriend coming down the street?
    a. admire her
    b. look the other way
    c. hide back the tears

15. In *Go Now,* what have the Moody Blues already said to their girlfriend?

a. I love you
b. goodbye
c. I'll call you tomorrow

16. What time of day is it that Marianne Faithful is watching the children play *As Tears Go By*?
    a. afternoon
    b. morning
    c. evening

17. According to Billy J. Kramer and the Dakotas in *Bad to Me*, why won't the birds in the sky be sad and lonely?
    a. the sun is shining bright
    b. they're together with their girlfriend
    c. there's love in the air

18. The Dave Clark Five yell *Catch Us If You Can* when they've got to get a move on and there's no more time for ___.
    a. wasting
    b. signing autographs
    c. fun

19. In *Baby, Now That I've Found You*, why are the Foundations lamenting after having found their perfect mate?
    a. they've discovered that you're already engaged
    b. you've told them you want to leave them
    c. you're beginning to treat them like yesterday's news

20. In *It's My Life*, although the Animals are dressed in rags, what do they say they'll wear one day?
    a. sable
    b. clothes
    c. leather

21. In *Time of the Season*, what question do the Zombies ask their prospective love-mate?
    a. Are you lonesome?
    b. Have you ever met someone so hot before?
    c. Who's your daddy?

22. When did Herman's Hermits say they first passed by and saw two *Silhouettes* on the shade?
    a. last week
    b. early this morning
    c. last night

23. When the Left Banke had a date with a *Pretty Ballerina*, how did her hair look?
    a. tangled and knotted
    b. brilliant
    c. heavenly

24. In *The Last Time*, even though the Rolling Stones say they told their girlfriend once and then twice, what did she never do?
    a. listen to their advice
    b. melt their heart of ice
    c. cure them of their lice

25. In *Sunshine Superman*, through what did the sunshine come for Donovan today?
    a. your eyes
    b. his window
    c. the rain

26. In *A World Without Love*, until Peter and Gordon can see their true love smile, what do they want you to do to them?
    a. laugh at them
    b. give them your sympathy
    c. lock them away

27. Where did Van Morrison and his *Brown-Eyed Girl* go when the rains came?

    a. to his room

    b. down in the hollow

    c. into the classroom

28. Petula Clark says it's *A Sign of the Times* that you tell your friends she's ___.

    a. your one and only

    b. a secret lover

    c. your long-lost sister

29. Tom Jones says that nowadays *It's Not Unusual* to see him do what?

    a. sing for nickels and dimes

    b. cry

    c. call your name in the night

30. In *Set Me Free*, if the Kinks can't have you to themselves, who do they have left?

    a. only themselves

    b. their dream lover

    c. no one

31. The Barbarians say in *Are You a Boy or Are You a Girl* that with your long blond hair, you're either a girl or you come from ___.

    a. Liverpool

    b. San Francisco

    c. Laguna Beach

32. In *Friday on My Mind*, where are the Easybeats planning to have fun?

    a. on the beach

    b. in their room

    c. in the city

33. In *Shapes*, what do the Yardbirds wonder might happen to them when tomorrow comes?
    a. Will they be bolder than today?
    b. Will you still love them?
    c. What will be the shape of the world?

34. As a token of her appreciation *To Sir With Love*, Lulu would like for him to ___.
    a. let her give her heart to him
    b. give her an A
    c. let her take him on a summer vacation

35. Gerry and the Pacemakers offer reassurance that *I'll Be There* when all your dreams are ___.
    a. coming true
    b. broken
    c. paying off

36. In *Glad All Over*, even though other girls may try to take them away from you, where do the Dave Clark Five still plan to stay?
    a. at your doorstep
    b. in your heart
    c. by your side

37. When they *Paint It Black*, what don't the Rolling Stones want to see anymore?
    a. colors
    b. anything
    c. your face

38. Although Eric Burdon and the Animals say in *San Franciscan Nights* that they weren't born there, what do they add might happen?
    a. perhaps they'll die there
    b. they might retire there
    c. they may return in a future life there

39. With *No Milk Today,* what do Herman's Hermits say this message marks the end of?

   a. their job

   b. their dreams

   c. an era

40. In *I'm a Man,* what is it that the Spencer Davis Group can't help but do?

   a. love you

   b. walk tall

   c. feel jealousy

41. What happened in *I Started a Joke* when the Bee Gees began to cry?

   a. everyone got up and left

   b. everyone else began to cry

   c. the whole world started laughing

42. The Kinks teasingly say that the world envies *A Well Respected Man* because he does the best things in what manner?

   a. modestly

   b. conservatively

   c. self-servingly

43. According to Petula Clark, what can change *My Love?*

   a. your sweet words

   b. another girl

   c. nothing

44. Chad and Jeremy request *Willow Weep for Me* when the ___ fall.

   a. stars

   b. shadows

   c. teardrops

45. Why do the Rolling Stones say you can't hang a name on *Ruby Tuesday*?
  a. she goes by a dozen aliases
  b. she changes with every new day
  c. she'll make you regret it if you try

46. According to Donovan, what does the *Universal Soldier* think we'll someday put an end to?
  a. war
  b. communism
  c. poverty

47. How tall is Them's *Gloria*?
  a. 4'10"
  b. 5'4"
  c. 6'2"

48. What do the Animals say the *Sky Pilot* will never do?
  a. reach the sky
  b. come back down to earth
  c. become the solution for peace

49. When Herman's Hermits tell us *This Door Swings Both Ways*, how do they say we must see life in order to call ourselves complete?
  a. without fear
  b. from both sides
  c. as a completed mission

50. Although the Nashville Teens loathe *Tobacco Road*, what one word best describes what it means to them?
  a. hell
  b. pollution
  c. home

BONUS QUIZ

1. According to Eric Burdon and the Animals in *Monterey*, whose music made them cry?
    a. Ravi Shankar
    b. the Who
    c. Hugh Masakela

2. According to Hedgehopper's Anonymous in *It's Good-News Week*, what did someone drop somewhere?
    a. a bomb
    b. a letter
    c. their hopes and dreams

3. Though the Who say *I Can See for Miles*, what is it they claim you said they'd need to see through the haze?
    a. a spotlight
    b. a crystal ball
    c. a telescope

4. According to the Rolling Stones in *Sympathy for the Devil*, who really killed the Kennedys?
    a. you and me
    b. the CIA
    c. Oliver Stone

5. What do the Hollies want to have *Stop! Stop! Stop!* so they can have time to breathe?
    a. your constant nagging
    b. their suspicious thoughts
    c. the music

6. The Neon Philharmonic advises the *Morning Girl* to read her box of Cheerios, go out and ___.
    a. get a job

    b. find a man

    c. buy some milk

7. After having a *Double Shot,* how did the Swinging Medallions feel when they woke up the next morning?

    a. great

    b. tired

    c. bad

8. What kind of shows did Peter and Gordon's *Lady Godiva* perform in after she had achieved her fame?

    a. comedies

    b. striptease

    c. beauty pageants

9. In *Here Comes the Night,* what can Them see outside their window?

    a. their girlfriend walking with another guy

    b. the darkness settling in

    c. children playing in the park

10. In *A Summer Song,* what will remind Chad and Jeremy of summer days and of you?

    a. the warmth of the summer rays

    b. the rain falling upon the window pane

    c. the birds in the trees

11. In *Catch the Wind,* what would Donovan do if he were able to love you now?

    a. fly to the stars

    b. rush to your house

    c. sing

12. In *What's New Pussycat?* what part does Tom Jones want to make contact with?

    a. your nose

    b. your heart

    c. your tongue

13. According to Unit Four Plus Two in *Concrete and Clay*, their love will never die even if the concrete and clay beneath their feet ____.

    a. melts

    b. leads them on another path

    c. begins to crumble

14. How old were the Animals when they smoked their first cigarette in *When I Was Young*?

    a. fourteen

    b. two

    c. ten

15. What treat do Billy J. Kramer and the Dakotas offer to the *Little Children* if they'll just go away?

    a. twenty-five cents

    b. a peak

    c. an ice-cream cone

16. According to Four Jacks and a Jill in *Master Jack*, what word describes the world they live in?

    a. exciting

    b. strange

    c. wonderful

17. In *I Know a Place*, how does Petula Clark describe the lighting of this hideaway?

    a. psychedelic

    b. sensuous and inviting

    c. always low

18. In *You Turn Me On*, what dance does Ian Whitcomb want you to do with him?

    a. the twist

    b. the jerk

    c. the dog

19. In *It's Gonna Be All Right,* why do Gerry and the Pacemakers say they'll stay close by your side?
    a. to keep you satisfied
    b. so love can be your guide
    c. so you won't run and hide

20. According to the Seekers in *I'll Never Find Another You,* there's a new world somewhere that is called ___.
    a. paradise
    b. Love City
    c. the promised land

American Pop
(1950s-1990s)

Pop has always been a favorite form of rock and roll for many fans. From the biggest hits of Bobby Darin up to the latest hits of Paul Simon and Billy Joel, pop has kept fingers snapping and feet tapping to the lyrically rich and oftentimes sobering beat of the times.

QUIZ A

1. When Neil Sedaka's *Happy Birthday Sweet Sixteen* was six years old, Neil was her ___.
   a. enemy
   b. babysitter
   c. big brother

2. How does the 5th Dimension want you to get down to the *Stoned Soul Picnic*?
   a. by surrey
   b. on a jet
   c. anyway you can

3. The O'Jays say that although they smile at you, what do the *Back Stabbers* really want to do?
   a. cut you up into pieces
   b. spit on you
   c. take your place

4. Now that *Sunday Will Never Be the Same*, what kind of weather do Spanky and Our Gang predict?
   a. hail
   b. rain
   c. sunny skies

5. Because you keep pushing her love over the *Borderline*, how does Madonna feel?
   a. like a whole new world is about to begin
   b. like she's going to lose her mind
   c. like a virgin

6. In *Cat's in the Cradle*, what did Harry Chapin's son say he wanted to do when he grew up?
   a. be just like his dad
   b. drive his dad's car
   c. have a son that would look up to him, too

7. In *Sweet Caroline*, how many people does Neil Diamond say it takes to fill up the night?
   a. two
   b. as many as the room can hold
   c. one

8. Jim Croce's *Bad, Bad Leroy Brown* is meaner than a ____.
   a. skunk
   b. wild cat
   c. junkyard dog

9. In *It Never Rains in California*, in what direction was the 747 that Albert Hammond got on headed?
   a. east
   b. west
   c. north

10. What do Sly and the Family Stone enjoy in the country sun as part of their *Hot Fun in the Summertime*?

a. a picnic
b. the game of love
c. a county fair

11. In *American Pie*, what car did Don McLean drive to the levy, which he found to be dry?
a. a Ford Mustang
b. a Chevy
c. a Cadillac

12. Paul Anka says that because *(You're) Having My Baby*, what does this tell him?
a. that you'll be his forever
b. you forgot to take the pill
c. how much you love him

13. In *Will You Be There*, what does Michael Jackson want you to hold him like?
a. the Jordan river
b. a mother with her baby
c. a child with her teddy bear

14. According to Bobby Darin, until he finds his *Dream Lover* what is all that he can do?
a. keep calling and searching
b. go to sleep and dream again
c. learn to do it by himself

15. Now that Cat Stevens has lost everything to his friend in *Wild World*, what does she now want to do?
a. open a cookie business
b. move to the country
c. start something new

16. Jerry Butler says in *He Will Break Your Heart* that the other boy doesn't love you the way ___.
a. a boy should

    b. he loves you

    c. you want to be loved

17. In *I Got You Babe*, how do Sonny and Cher rationalize the fact that their money is spent before it is even earned?

    a. in that way, there won't ever be a reason to hire lawyers after the divorce

    b. it's a sign of the times

    c. in that way, they won't ever fight

18. What problem is caused for B. J. Thomas as *Raindrops Keep Falling on My Head*?

    a. he's drowning in love

    b. nothing seems to fit

    c. he can't stop the rain from falling

19. In *Oh How Happy*, how many times have the Shades of Blue kissed your lips?

    a. dozens

    b. a thousand

    c. none

20. In *Walk on By*, what does Dionne Warwick do each time she sees you?

    a. cry

    b. look the other way

    c. throw up

21. In *Gypsies, Tramps, and Thieves*, where does Cher say she was born?

    a. in the backseat of a pickup truck

    b. in a tenement slum

    c. in a wagon

22. In *Indiana Wants Me*, what did R. Dean Taylor see around him that indicated he had been discovered?

    a. flashing red lights

    b. six white horses

    c. flying saucers

23. In *Kodachrome*, Paul Simon says his lack of education hasn't hurt him because he is able to read what?
    a. enough to get by
    b. the writing on the wall
    c. his name and yours

24. The Spinners say *I'll Be Around* even if they have to ——.
    a. plead
    b. leave
    c. crawl

25. In *I'm So Excited*, how do the Pointer Sisters feel knowing that they're about to lose control?
    a. they like it
    b. they're afraid of what they might do
    c. they're nervous and uncertain

26. In *Just the Way You Are*, what does Billy Joel want to be sure of?
    a. that you'll always be the same person that he's known
    b. that you really love him
    c. that you don't plan to gain weight

27. According to Nicolette Larson, what is it going to take a *Lotta Love* to do?
    a. change the way things are
    b. make her happy
    c. satisfy her desire

28. When you find that hope is gone, where does Mariah Carey say you will find the *Hero*?
    a. inside yourself
    b. up above
    c. in a song

29. According to the Sanford/Townsend Band, what is all amist from the *Smoke From a Distant Fire*?

a. their desire
b. the rooftops
c. their lady's eyes

30. According to Gerry Rafferty in *Baker Street*, the city has so many people but what does it not have?
    a. soul
    b. proper housing
    c. enough protection

31. In *Sunny*, what does Bobby Hebb say about how he felt yesterday?
    a. he didn't have a care in the world
    b. love for him was such an easy game to play
    c. his life was filled with rain

32. In *Baby, the Rain Must Fall*, what leads Glenn Yarbrough to where he must go?
    a. his heart
    b. his job
    c. destiny

33. In *Can't Take My Eyes Off You*, how does the sight of you leave Frankie Valli?
    a. satisfied
    b. weak
    c. craving more

34. What did Robert Knight do to ruin his *Everlasting Love*?
    a. he went away
    b. he embarrassed her
    c. he cheated on her

35. What do the Osmonds say about *One Bad Apple*?
    a. it makes everyone else look good
    b. it doesn't spoil the whole bunch
    c. it's looking for another bad apple

36. Although Linda Scott says *I've Told Every Little Star*, who is it that she hasn't told?

    a. you
    b. her guardian angel
    c. any other person

37. Until the time Madonna says she will *Live to Tell* the thousand lies she has heard, what does she say will happen to these secrets?

    a. they'll become rumors
    b. they'll burn inside of her
    c. she'll write them in her diary

38. What is Neil Sedaka doing while he hears *Laughter in the Rain*?

    a. walking hand in hand with one he loves
    b. looking outside his lonely window
    c. taking a shower

39. Yvonne Elliman says that *If I Can't Have You*, who will she want?

    a. your little brother
    b. anyone who'll dance with her
    c. nobody

40. In *Hopelessly*, what does Rick Astley say he does every night?

    a. takes a cold shower
    b. takes a hot bath
    c. walks the wire

41. Although Stephanie Mills says *I Never Knew Love Like This Before*, what is it that she won't have anymore?

    a. another love like this
    b. loneliness
    c. reasons to doubt you

42. In *I Feel the Earth Move*, Carole King sees your face as mellow as which month?
    a. May
    b. July
    c. November

43. According to Chris Montez, *The More I See You* the more ___.
    a. he dreams of you
    b. he wants you
    c. he doesn't know you

44. What does Joe South say you should not do until you've been able to *Walk a Mile in My Shoes*?
    a. talk about him
    b. criticize him
    c. analyze him

45. What does Melissa Manchester suggest instead when she says *Don't Cry Out Loud*?
    a. keep it inside
    b. keep your mouth shut
    c. save it for a rainy day

46. In *You Can Call Me Al*, what does Paul Simon say you can be?
    a. his bodyguard
    b. his groupie
    c. a friend of his

47. Under what conditions does Gloria Gaynor say *I Will Survive*?
    a. if you love her
    b. without you by her side
    c. if the stars no longer shine

48. In *Hot Stuff*, what is Donna Summer eating?
    a. she hasn't eaten anything since she met you
    b. her heart out
    c. chili burritos

49. In *Physical*, what does Olivia Newton-John want to hear talk?

   a. your body
   b. your eyes
   c. her heart

50. In *Leave a Tender Moment Alone*, what does Billy Joel say about the feeling he has?

   a. it's not something he can deny
   b. it's the best feeling he's ever known
   c. it's like the feeling of spending a night back home

QUIZ B

1. Although the Spiral Staircase says they'll love you *More Today Than Yesterday*, how does this amount compare to how much they'll love you tomorrow?

   a. it won't compare
   b. only time will tell
   c. only half as much as tomorrow

2. To whom is R. B. Greaves's letter addressed in *Take a Letter, Maria*?

   a. his wife
   b. his lawyer
   c. Uncle Sam

3. According to Simon and Garfunkel, who loves *Mrs. Robinson* more than she will ever know?

   a. everyone
   b. Jesus
   c. all the kids

4. What one thing don't Spanky and Our Gang promise to do, even though *I'd Like to Get to Know You*?

   a. shower with you
   b. marry you
   c. love you

5. In *Don't Make Me Over*, Dionne Warwick wants to be loved even with all her ___.
   a. faults
   b. money
   c. other boyfriends

6. In *Up, Up and Away*, what does the 5th Dimension invite you to do?
   a. smoke some of their weed
   b. take a ride in their balloon
   c. sing along with them

7. In which month does Neil Sedaka call his *Calendar Girl* his little Valentine?
   a. February
   b. March
   c. every month

8. According to Jim Croce in you *Don't Mess With Jim*, what do friends call Jim when they talk about him?
   a. sucker
   b. mister
   c. boss

9. In *Everyday People*, what do Sly and the Family Stone say about their beliefs?
   a. they are expressed in their songs
   b. ain't nobody's business but their own
   c. they're the same for everyone

10. In *You're So Vain*, Carly Simon says that her male acquaintance walked into the party as though he were walking onto ___.
    a. a stage
    b. a yacht
    c. water

11. According to Bobby Darin, who disappeared just around the time *Mack the Knife* got back in town?
    a. his wife's lover

   b.   Louie Miller
   c.   Jackie Paper

12.   B. J. Thomas is *Hooked On a Feeling* that you're
      —.
      a.   in love with him
      b.   his kind of girl
      c.   dying to meet him

13.   According to Whitney Houston in *I Wanna Dance
      With Somebody*, what happens when the darkness
      approaches?
      a.   she can't see straight
      b.   she begins to dream about you
      c.   loneliness calls

14.   In *Could've Been*, what does Tiffany say about the
      flowers you gave her?
      a.   they're just about to die
      b.   they're a symbol of your love for her
      c.   they're only imitations

15.   In *Reasons*, for how long do Earth, Wind and Fire
      want to love you?
      a.   one night
      b.   forever
      c.   until they run out of reasons to see you

16.   Michael Jackson advises you to *Beat It* and not try
      to be a —.
      a.   party-pooper
      b.   macho man
      c.   hero

17.   Where are the Pointer Sisters when they hear the
      radio and get filled with *Fire*?
      a.   under your bed
      b.   in your bed
      c.   in your car

18. What does Billy Joel say happens to us in *The River of Dreams?*
    a. we're all carried along
    b. we're all cleansed with purity
    c. we're all drowned in hope

19. According to Oliver in *Good Morning Starshine,* who greets the light by saying hello?
    a. he does
    b. the moon
    c. the earth

20. What does Jackie DeShannon say will happen if you *Put a Little Love in Your Heart?*
    a. there'll be none left in your soul
    b. the world will be a better place
    c. you'll live a lot longer

21. Where was Janis Joplin waiting for a train before becoming part of the traveling couple *Me and Bobby McGee?*
    a. Baton Rouge
    b. Cheyenne
    c. Tuscaloosa

22. In *Don't Leave Me This Way,* what does Thelma Houston say she can't do without your love?
    a. dream
    b. plan her future with you
    c. survive

23. Although no one makes her feel as you do, what does Diana Ross say in *Upside Down* that she knows you're doing?
    a. winning her heart
    b. cheating on her
    c. using mirrors to confuse her

24. According to Amii Stewart in *Knock on Wood,* what is better than any she's ever known before?

    a. the construction of her new house
    b. her faith in a brighter tomorrow
    c. your love

25. In *Hopelessly Devoted to You*, what does Olivia Newton-John say you think of her?
    a. that she's just a girl who lives next door
    b. that she's a fool who's willing to wait
    c. that she's an angel who has come to the rescue

26. Because you are her *Lucky Star*, what happens whenever Madonna thinks of you?
    a. she starts to glow
    b. she cries
    c. she feels lucky

27. In *That's the Way Love Goes*, what does Janet Jackson compare the attraction to?
    a. a moth to a flame
    b. a magnet to steel
    c. a bee to a flower

28. In *She Bop*, in what magazine did Cyndi Lauper see the new sensation in an ad?
    a. Playgirl
    b. Blonde Babes
    c. Blue Boy

29. Cat Stevens's *Peace Train* lies at the edge of ___.
    a. the tracks
    b. darkness
    c. your mind

30. What can't Harry Nilsson do *Without You*?
    a. make love
    b. live
    c. have a party

31. What is Honey Cone seeking in the *Want Ads*?
    a. a job

    b. a man that's true

    c. anything that's free

32. Although Madonna has cried so many times before, what does she say about those teardrops in *True Blue?*

    a. they hold the memories of love that can never return

    b. they were only tears of joy

    c. they won't fall again

33. When Paul Simon was uncertain about the *Fifty Ways to Leave Your Lover*, what did his mate tell Gus he should do?

    a. sleep on it

    b. talk it over

    c. get on a bus

34. Although Carole King and her boyfriend did try to make it, what happened to her so that *It's Too Late?*

    a. she married someone else

    b. something died deep inside

    c. she entered a convent

35. According to Tony Joe White in *Polk Salad Annie*, what does polk salad look like?

    a. a turnip green

    b. a zucchini

    c. shredded dollar bills

36. In *I Thank the Lord for the Nighttime*, what does Neil Diamond say about the daytime?

    a. it turns him off

    b. it's the time to be in the sun

    c. it's the time to call his baby

37. According to the Spinners in *Could It Be I'm Falling in Love*, meeting you was their ___.

    a. big mistake

    b. fortune

    c. destiny

38. In *Greatest Love of All*, what does Whitney Houston believe about the children?

    a. they are our future

    b. they are all one family

    c. they should be seen, not heard

39. What does Joe Jackson complain you want to do that seems to be *Breaking Us in Two*?

    a. go your own way

    b. become an actress

    c. things he can't do

40. In *Shame*, where does Evelyn "Champagne" King say she wants to be?

    a. on a desert island with you

    b. wrapped in your arms

    c. in a ring filled with mud

41. In *These Boots Are Made for Walking*, what does Nancy Sinatra say her boots are going to do?

    a. walk all over you

    b. get muddy listening to your lies

    c. walk her away from you

42. According to the Fifth Dimension in *Go Where You Wanna Go*, how many miles away did you travel?

    a. five hundred

    b. twenty

    c. three thousand

43. In *Breaking Up Is Hard to Do*, how will Neil Sedaka feel if you leave?

    a. blue

    b. mad

    c. relieved

44. Even though Barbara Mason says *Yes, I'm Ready* to learn, what does she say she doesn't know how to do?
    a. drive
    b. say sweet nothin's
    c. kiss your lips

45. What does Bobby Darin say he wasn't privy to in *Splish Splash*?
    a. that someone had turned off the heat
    b. that he was being robbed
    c. that there was a party going on

46. As Jim Croce is speaking with the *Operator*, with whom does he tell her that his ex-girlfriend is living?
    a. the operator's husband
    b. his ex-friend Ray
    c. her parents

47. In *Hey, Little Devil*, Neil Sedaka warns his mischievous friend that she's met her ___.
    a. future lover
    b. match
    c. Waterloo

48. When Sly and the Family Stone say *I Want to Take You Higher*, what do they want you to do to them?
    a. get stoned with them
    b. light their fire
    c. go mountain biking

49. Although Neil Diamond's *Cherry Cherry* loves him, when is he going to show her how he feels about her?
    a. tonight
    b. not until he's good and ready
    c. tomorrow morning

50. If you want Tony Orlando and Dawn to be with you, where should you *Knock Three Times?*
    a. in their heart
    b. on the bed
    c. on the ceiling

BONUS QUIZ

1. In *This Time the Girl Is Gonna Stay,* with what does B. J. Thomas's heart beat?
    a. the ticking of the clock
    b. the rhythm of her sigh
    c. the sound of her heartbeat

2. According to Matt Monro, when one is *Born Free* what is life good for?
    a. living
    b. nothing
    c. falling in love

3. In *Still Crazy After All These Years,* what does Paul Simon say about love songs that whisper in his ears?
    a. they're what he longs for
    b. he can't understand what they're trying to say
    c. he's not a fool for them

4. Because Joe Jackson is so tired of the darkness in his life, what does he suggest doing to go *Steppin' Out?*
    a. putting on your dancing shoes
    b. driving in a car
    c. turning on the light

5. According to Paul McCartney in *The Girl Is Mine,* what does Michael Jackson send to the girl, something that Paul considers only a waste of time?
    a. letters

    b. autographed pictures and a scarf
    c. roses and his dreams

6. During what month was it that Al Stewart felt himself go drifting into *Time Passages?*
    a. July
    b. December
    c. March

7. In *Do You Know the Way to San Jose*, Dionne Warwick wants to return there from which city?
    a. Atlanta
    b. Brooklyn
    c. Los Angeles

8. What is the astrological alignment of the moon in the Fifth Dimension's *Aquarius/Let the Sunshine In?*
    a. it's at a total eclipse
    b. it's aligned with Mars
    c. it's in the seventh house

9. In Sonny and Cher's *Baby Don't Go*, how long has Cher been in town?
    a. a month
    b. a year
    c. eighteen years

10. When does Simon and Garfunkel's *I Am a Rock* take place?
    a. August
    b. November
    c. December

11. As a final tribute in *Ode to Billy Joe*, what does Bobbie Gentry drop to the muddy water below?
    a. her love letters
    b. a mint
    c. her body

12. Dionne Warwick says that *Anyone Who Had a Heart* would do what to her?
    a. forgive her
    b. come back and never leave her
    c. take her in his arms

13. In *Jackson*, Nancy Sinatra and Lee Hazlewood got married in a fever that was hotter than ___.
    a. a peppered sprout
    b. the blazing sun
    c. a dog in heat

14. In *Bad Blood*, what does Neil Sedaka say the woman does with the wink of an eye?
    a. makes promises she can't keep
    b. robs you blind
    c. captures your heart

15. Where does Donna Summer say the *Bad Girls* are at night?
    a. at her house acting bad
    b. on the dance floor
    c. on the street

16. What does Diana Ross say about any cure for her *Love Hangover*?
    a. she should have had it yesterday
    b. she doesn't want it
    c. it's in your kiss

17. According to Olivia Newton-John, what shines in *Xanadu*?
    a. the neon lights
    b. the stars up above
    c. your eyes

18. Where does Hot say the *Angel in Your Arms* is going to be tonight?

a.   in the arms of someone else
b.   deep in your heart
c.   in your midnight fantasies

19.   What does Janet Jackson ask herself time and time *Again*?
a.   Are you going to notice her?
b.   What will it take for others to respect her for being herself?
c.   How can she be strong?

20.   In *All This Time*, what does Tiffany say hearts are good for?
a.   breaking
b.   jokes and artichokes
c.   souvenirs

Dance / Party Rock
(1960s-1990s)

Dance/party rock has become rock and roll's most commercially successful offshoot, starting back when Chubby Checker used a towel to introduce his new dance, the twist. We've celebrated our best times to the sounds of dance tracks, taking a brief tour through bubblegum music, a lengthier stopover into discomania, and finally coming full circle to the eclectic eighties and nineties, replete with stars from DeBarge to Paula Abdul to Gloria Estefan. If one thing can be said for rock and roll, it's that the *Rhythm Is Gonna Get You,* and nowhere is it more evident than in dance/party rock!

QUIZ A

1. In *Cool Jerk,* when others look at the Capitols as if they're fools, they know that deep inside the people know they're ___.
   a. crazy
   b. hip
   c. cool

2. Chubby Checker is going to do *The Twist* until what happens?
   a. their folks come home
   b. they get too tired to twist anymore
   c. they tear the house down

3. In *Do You Want to Dance*, what does Bobby Freeman want you to do as a prelude to hopefully making romance?
   a. take off your shoes
   b. whisper in his ear
   c. squeeze him

4. While at *Palisades Park*, where were they when Freddy Cannon gave his girl a hug?
   a. in the tunnel of love
   b. on the top of the ferris wheel
   c. at the ticket counter

5. Why wouldn't the *Purple People Eater* eat Sheb Wooley?
   a. they were friends eternally
   b. he was too tough
   c. he wasn't purple

6. The Larks report that when you do *The Jerk*, what moves so fine?
   a. your legs
   b. your hips
   c. your eyes

7. Although *Valleri* is the same person who used to hang around the Monkees' door, what has changed?
   a. her looks
   b. her personality
   c. her name

8. According to the Cowsills, why is their *Hair* so long?
   a. there's no barber shop in town
   b. they don't know
   c. so they can speak their mind

9. In *Night Fever*, what parts of the Bee Gees are affected by the girl moving across the floor?
   a. their hands and feet
   b. their tongues and lips
   c. their minds and souls

10. Where does Andy Gibb want to do his *Shadow Dancing?*
    a. under the moonlight
    b. across the floor
    c. anywhere he's alone

11. What does Heatwave say about the *Boogie Nights?*
    a. they're the best in town
    b. they're hot
    c. they're not as warm as the boogie days

12. According to Foxy in *Get Off*, what makes a lady find out what she wants in a man?
    a. danger and excitement
    b. a special kiss
    c. jealousy and desire

13. In *I Want Your Love*, what is it that Chic asks if you've ever wanted to try to see how well it fits?
    a. your answers to their questions
    b. their love
    c. their clothes

14. In *Love Machine*, who do the Miracles say they want to work for?
    a. Uncle Sam
    b. Venus, the goddess of love
    c. nobody but you

15. Where does KC and the Sunshine Band say you should *(Shake, Shake, Shake) Shake Your Booty?*

    a. on the dance floor
    b. outside their doorstep
    c. anywhere you want

16. When does Gloria Estefan and the Miami Sound Machine say the *Rhythm Is Gonna Get You?*
    a. when you reach the dance floor
    b. tonight
    c. when you take them home

17. Paula Abdul says he's *Cold Hearted* because he doesn't ___.
    a. play by the rules
    b. warm up to her
    c. know love at all

18. Because *She Works Hard for the Money,* what does Donna Summer say you better do?
    a. give her respect
    b. pay her on time
    c. treat her right

19. After tiring of the status-symbol land of *Pleasant Valley Sunday,* what do the Monkees want?
    a. a girl to love
    b. a change of scenery
    c. to blow it up and start again

20. According to the Trashmen in *Surfin' Bird*, what is "the word"?
    a. bird
    b. surf
    c. cowabunga

21. Now that *School Is Out,* what does Gary U.S. Bonds just have time to do?
    a. take his girl out on a date
    b. hand in the final exam
    c. go surfing

22. According to the Dovells, how exciting are the kids in Bristol when they do the *Bristol Stomp*?
    a. they're boring compared to the kids in Liverpool
    b. they are sharp as a pistol
    c. they are so exciting, they have to close the club early every night

23. Little Eva says that doing the *Loco-Motion* is easier than ___.
    a. learning the ABC's
    b. going to school
    c. doing the twist

24. According to the Royal Guardsmen in *Snoopy Versus the Red Baron*, how many men died trying to end the spree of the Red Baron?
    a. eighty
    b. twenty
    c. two hundred

25. Although other people say in *Hey, Hey, We're the Monkees* that the pre-fab foursome just want to cause problems by monkeying around, how do the Monkees respond?
    a. they're just normal people who like hanging upside down
    b. that's what they're here for, but don't let that get you down
    c. they're too busy singing to put anybody down

26. In *Straight Up*, what does Paula Abdul want to know?
    a. if you're going to love her forever
    b. if you're going to wake up
    c. if you're really straight

27. In *I Love the Nightlife*, what doesn't Alicia Bridges want you to talk about tonight?

a. love
b. leaving
c. your wife

28. In *How Deep Is Your Love*, although people are trying to break you apart from the Bee Gees, what do the Bee Gees say others should do?
   a. mind their own business
   b. leave you alone and let you and them be together
   c. find their own lovers

29. Because the feeling's right and the music's tight, what does GQ recommend for you to do in *Disco Nights (Rock Freak)*?
   a. get up
   b. find a dance partner
   c. light up

30. According to Shannon in *Let the Music Play*, when did love put them into a groove?
   a. as soon as they started to move
   b. as soon as they set eyes on you
   c. when they knew they had something to prove

31. In *Rock the Boat*, what does Hues Corporation say has saved them from the rolling seas?
   a. the island of love
   b. a little bit of luck
   c. your arms

32. According to Salt 'n' Pepa in *Push It*, who's this dance meant for?
   a. everyone
   b. those who like to take it to the limit
   c. only the sexy people

33. In *Shake Your Groove Thing*, what do Peaches and Herb want to show the world?

a. they can dance
b. their love is real
c. dreams can come true

34. According to the Trammps, how tall is the *Disco Inferno?*
    a. five feet ten inches
    b. one hundred stories
    c. as high as heaven

35. What word does Brick use to describe their *Music?*
    a. hot
    b. proper
    c. funky

36. In *Boogie Fever*, what happened when the Sylvers took their girlfriend to the drive-in show?
    a. she left them for another guy
    b. she turned down the speaker
    c. they vowed to love one another until the end of time

37. According to Sam Cooke, who is the man in evening clothes *Twistin' the Night Away* with?
    a. a chick in slacks
    b. a poor man's lady
    c. a girl with no name

38. In *Do You Love Me*, why weren't the Contours loved?
    a. they had an attitude
    b. they couldn't dance
    c. nobody knew they existed

39. Along with the Zombies, who else appeared at Bobby "Boris" Pickett's *Monster Mash?*
    a. Frankenstein
    b. Godzilla
    c. Dracula

40. Where does Chris Kenner say the dance-hall named *I Like It Like That* is located?

   a. in Tucson
   b. across the track
   c. in Hackensack

41. According to the Crests, the *Sixteen Candles* on their young friend's birthday cake are not as bright as ___.

   a. her eyes
   b. the stars in the sky
   c. their dreams

42. What famous place does Freddie Cannon invite everyone down to in *Where the Action Is?*

   a. the Sunset Strip
   b. Greenwich Village
   c. Palisades Park

43. What does Larry Vern want *Mr. Custer* to realize regarding his readiness to go to battle?

   a. he's ready, willing, and able
   b. he'll follow 'til his dying day
   c. he doesn't want to go

44. What is it the Orlons say doesn't happen in the twist that you can do in *The Watusi?*

   a. you can get kissed
   b. you can get down and dirty
   c. you can fall in love

45. Who did Bobby Day's *Rockin' Robin* go steady with?

   a. the buzzard
   b. a raven
   c. another robin

46. Buddy Knox says that if you'll be his *Party Doll,* what will he do in return?

    a. pay you handsomely
    b. be your puppet
    c. make love to you

47. Who does the Hollywood Argyle's *Alley-Oop* have as a chauffeur?

    a. his woman
    b. a dinosaur
    c. a bear-cat

48. In *Hello Mudduh, Hello Fadduh,* what is the name of the camp where Allan Sherman is staying?

    a. Camp Chimachonga
    b. Camp Ulysses
    c. Camp Granada

49. Who do *Those Oldies but Goodies* remind Little Caesar and the Romans of?

    a. you
    b. the person they used to be
    c. their friends

50. In *Beep Beep,* what model car is trying to pass the Playmates' Cadillac?

    a. a Rabbit
    b. a Rambler
    c. a Pinto

QUIZ B

  1. In *Let the Little Girl Dance,* with whom does Billy Bland say she wants to dance?

    a. him
    b. you
    c. anybody

  2. Dee Dee Sharp is going to *Ride* her pony until what happens?

a. you're by her side
b. she falls off
c. they stop the carousel

3. In *Daydream Believer*, what time does the alarm awaken the Monkees?
   a. 7:00
   b. 6:00
   c. noon

4. Who did the Cowsills meet in *The Rain, the Park, and Other Things*?
   a. a flower girl
   b. a long-lost friend
   c. a devil woman

5. How does *Mony Mony* make Tommy James and the Shondells feel?
   a. cheap and dirty
   b. so good
   c. hungry for love

6. In *Do Ya Wanna Get Funky With Me*, what did Peter Brown realize when he saw the fire in her eyes?
   a. the flame was just for him
   b. she was the devil in disguise
   c. he was on fire

7. Where does Michael Sembello say she's a *Maniac*?
   a. in bed
   b. behind the wheel
   c. on the floor

8. According to Frankie Valli, *Grease* is a word that's
   ——.
   a. got a groove
   b. hard to handle
   c. got a new meaning

9. In *We Are Family,* who does Sister Sledge say she has with her?
    a. all her friends
    b. only her lonely self
    c. all her sisters

10. In *Keep It Comin' Love*, what doesn't KC and the Sunshine Band want you to do?
    a. reach for a new shining star
    b. continue quarreling
    c. let the well run dry

11. When A Taste of Honey says that you are no exception in *Boogie, Oogie, Oogie*, what do they say you've got to do just like everyone else?
    a. be cool
    b. boogie on the floor
    c. take off your clothes

12. In *I Think I Love You*, why is the Partridge Family afraid of being in love?
    a. they don't know if their girlfriend has been tested
    b. they're not sure it'll be their true love
    c. they're not sure of a love there is no cure for

13. When Chris Montez suggests *Let's Dance*, what three dances does he specifically offer for your selection?
    a. the twist, stomp, and mashed potato
    b. the frug, fly, and Watusi
    c. the tango, mambo, and samba

14. In what city did Archie Bell and the Drells say they've just started a new dance called the *Tighten Up*?
    a. Spokane
    b. Pittsburgh
    c. Houston

15. What is the dance Bobby Freeman compares his dance with in *Do the Swim?*
    a. the hully gully
    b. the alligator
    c. the Charleston

16. Who does Jimmy Soul suggest for you to pick as your wife *If You Want to Be Happy?*
    a. Venus in blue jeans
    b. a younger girl
    c. an ugly girl

17. The Archies call their *Sugar, Sugar* their ___.
    a. party animal
    b. candy girl
    c. bedtime fantasy

18. According to the Royal Guardsmen in *Snoopy's Christmas*, what did the Red Baron cry out to Snoopy after he made Snoopy land behind the enemy lines?
    a. Merry Christmas!
    b. So long, hound dog!
    c. We're even, my friend!

19. What is it the Monkees don't want to do in *A Little Bit Me, A Little Bit You?*
    a. fight
    b. leave
    c. compromise

20. According to Chic, what is *Le Freak?*
    a. a French psychopath
    b. a new dance craze
    c. their boyfriend's new nickname

21. By wanting to *Get Down Tonight*, what do KC and the Sunshine Band suggest to do?

    a. lie on the floor and fall asleep
    b. party
    c. dance and make love

22. In *An Everlasting Love*, what did Andy Gibb know even before he first held you tight in his arms?
    a. that you would be his forever
    b. that he was losing you
    c. that you were his first love

23. Where is Linear *Sending All My Love*?
    a. to outer space
    b. to nobody
    c. to you

24. When Bruce Channel says *Hey! Baby*, what does he want to know?
    a. if you'll be his girl
    b. if he looks sexy
    c. your name

25. In *Monkey Time*, what does Major Lance say about the origin of the monkey dance?
    a. it began with a cat named Sloppy Joe
    b. he doesn't know how it started
    c. it began a long time ago

26. According to Hank Ballard and the Midnighters in *Finger Poppin' Time*, what is a real good sign?
    a. that they feel so good
    b. watch out for deer crossing
    c. that it's still early

27. When Maurice Williams and the Zodiacs ask you to *Stay*, how do your folks feel according to Maurice?
    a. filled with rage
    b. they wonder what's going to happen
    c. they don't mind

28. What do the Cowsills say you can rent while you're at *Indian Lake*?
   a. a loin cloth and feathers
   b. a tepee
   c. a canoe

29. KC and the Sunshine Band say *That's the Way (I Like It)* when you tell them what?
   a. you want to dance all night
   b. they're your loving man
   c. you're staying with them tonight

30. In *I Feel Love*, what does Donna Summer say about it?
   a. it's hot
   b. it's never felt this way before
   c. it's so good

31. Bobby McFerrin says to *Don't Worry Be Happy* even when the landlord says what?
   a. the rent is late
   b. your apartment has been burglarized
   c. it's time to move on

32. According to Gary U.S. Bonds, what flower is blooming down in *New Orleans*?
   a. the honeysuckle
   b. the poppy
   c. the chrysanthemum

33. In what street is it that the Dovells say *You Can't Sit Down*?
   a. any street with music
   b. South Street
   c. Love Street

34. What did the *Witch Doctor* give David Seville to win his girl's heart?
   a. a love potion

    b. a magical spell

    c. the right words to say

35. In *(I'm Not Your) Steppin' Stone*, the Monkees claim the clothes their girlfriend is wearing are causing ___.

    a. public scenes

    b. the weather to change

    c. earthquakes

36. What is Allan Sherman going to do with all the presents he has received during the *Twelve Days of Christmas?*

    a. donate them

    b. eat them

    c. exchange them

37. When does Peter Brown say you should *Dance With Me?*

    a. now

    b. when they play the music tight

    c. when you're through dancing with all the other guys

38. In *Stayin' Alive*, what can you tell by the way the Bee Gees use their walk?

    a. they're a woman's man

    b. they limp

    c. they can dance any way they want

39. According to Smokey Robinson and the Miracles, who's *Going to a Go Go?*

    a. they are

    b. all their friends

    c. everybody

40. According to Steam in *Na Na Hey Hey Kiss Him Goodbye*, your other boyfriend never loved you the way ___.

    a. they love you
    b. he loves all the other girls
    c. that made you beg for more

41. What does the Ohio Express have in its tummy that is so *Yummy Yummy Yummy*?
    a. mashed potatoes and green-eyed peas
    b. an appetite for seeing you
    c. love

42. What is the first thing Chubby Checker says you should do in the *Limbo Rock*?
    a. spread your feet
    b. bend back
    c. turn on the music

43. What does the *Bad Boy* do to the Miami Sound Machine?
    a. he beats them up at night
    b. he makes them feel so good
    c. he makes them jealous

44. Paula Abdul says she'd be *Forever Your Girl* even if another boy promises her what?
    a. the world
    b. all his money
    c. that he'll be true forever

45. In *Bottle of Wine*, where do the Fireballs want to go?
    a. to a bar
    b. home
    c. to your house

46. What are two dances Cannibal and the Head Hunters refer to in *Land of 1000 Dances*?
    a. swim and frug
    b. slop and fly
    c. pony and twist

47. According to the Jackson Five, how is their *Dancing Machine* built?

   a. sleek and fine

   b. with a space-age design

   c. tall and mean

48. According to Gary U.S. Bonds in *Dear Lady Twist*, if you do the twist what will happen to you?

   a. you will fall in love

   b. they will twist along with you

   c. you will never grow old

49. In *Get On Up*, what do the Esquires want to do with you?

   a. dance

   b. wake you up

   c. tie you to the bed

50. On what street do Joey Dee and the Starliters want you to go to meet the other fans of *The Peppermint Twist*?

   a. 7th Avenue

   b. South Street

   c. 45th Street

BONUS QUIZ

1. What is the name of the girl who was *Barefootin'* at Robert Parker's party?

   a. Suzie Q

   b. Long Tall Sally

   c. Alice

2. In Shirley Ellis's *The Name Game*, what is one name mentioned that is contrary to the general rules of the game?

   a. Lincoln

   b. Fred
   c. Nick

3. According to the members of Freez in *I.O.U.*, what do they sometimes cry?
   a. A-E-I-O-U
   b. they'll love you forever
   c. they'll pay you back with interest

4. Because these are *Good Times*, what does Chic say to do?
   a. forget about false promises
   b. leave your cares behind
   c. enjoy the moment

5. In *Pony Time*, Chubby Checker says to turn to your left when he says "gee" and turn to your right when he says ___?
   a. yeah
   b. whoa
   c. halt

6. Name one thing Sam Cooke says you should *Shake* your body like?
   a. a rattlesnake
   b. a hula hoop
   c. a bowl of soup

7. According to Claudine Clark, what colors are the *Party Lights*?
   a. red, blue, and green
   b. pink and gold
   c. orange and yellow

8. In *Turn the Beat Around*, what does Vicki Sue Robinson love to hear?
   a. words of love
   b. percussion
   c. your name

9. In *He's the Greatest Dancer,* in which city was Sister Sledge cruising with her gang?
   - **a.** San Francisco
   - **b.** Detroit
   - **c.** New York

10. Because he's found *Heaven on the 7th Floor,* what does Paul Nicholas not want you to do?
    - **a.** rescue him
    - **b.** bring him down
    - **c.** say goodbye

11. Although it's the Twister who is flying high in *Let's Twist Again,* what else does Chubby Checker ask if it is?
    - **a.** Superman
    - **b.** a bird
    - **c.** a tornado

12. In *Wooly Bully,* what do Sam the Sham and the Pharaohs ask us to learn to do?
    - **a.** treat animals with respect
    - **b.** dance
    - **c.** say please

13. In *Quarter to Three,* what is the name of the swingingest band Gary U.S. Bonds is dancing to?
    - **a.** the Dovells
    - **b.** Daddy G
    - **c.** the Comets

14. On what night is Ernie Maresca going crazy as he goes to *Shout, Shout?*
    - **a.** Friday
    - **b.** Thursday
    - **c.** Saturday

15. In *A Lover's Holiday,* how did the members of Change feel right before they met a man who asked whether he'd seen them before?

    a. excited
    b. lonely
    c. scared

16. In *You're the One That I Want*, what does Olivia Newton-John tell John Travolta?
    a. she's forever his girl
    b. she'll wait for him to return
    c. he better shape up

17. According to DeBarge in *Rhythm of the Night*, what is this not the night for doing?
    a. staying home
    b. talking
    c. fussing and fighting

18. In *Shout*, the Isley Brothers still remember when you used to be how young?
    a. three years old
    b. just a tiny baby
    c. nine years old

19. In *Let It Out (Let It All Hang Out)*, because the Hombres' television is on the blink, how does Galileo now look?
    a. fuzzy
    b. like a Boy Scout
    c. like their sister

20. When you take the *Last Train to Clarksville*, by what time do the Monkees say you'll be arriving?
    a. 7:00
    b. 4:30
    c. midnight

Contemporary American Rock
(1970s-1990s)

American rock since the 1970s has taken on many different faces, but as Billy Joel said in his pop classic, "It's all rock and roll to me." Three Dog Night ruled the land in the early seventies, Darryl Hall and John Oates, America, the Eagles, and the Steve Miller Band were ripe examples of later 1970s megastars; and can anyone overlook the rise to stardom of Bruce Springsteen and Prince? It seems we've traveled light years from the times of bobby socks and blue jeans, but is Jon Bon Jovi really so different from Elvis? Indeed, it's all rock and roll, alive and well in the good old USA.

QUIZ A

1. Before Gene Chandler first met his girlfriend in *Groovy Situation*, how were both feeling?
   a. in love
   b. happy
   c. lonely

2. In *Long Train Running*, the Doobie Brothers ask where you would be now without ___.
   a. railroad tracks
   b. love
   c. gas

3. According to the Righteous Brothers, if there's a *Rock and Roll Heaven*, they've got ___.
   a. a helluva band
   b. noise pollution
   c. no drummer

4. Because Bruce Springsteen says *I'm On Fire*, what can he do that no one else can do?
   a. fill all the girls with desire
   b. consume you in a flame of passion
   c. take you higher

5. What has Toto touched down in *Africa*?
   a. the rains
   b. the hearts of all the girls
   c. spiders and snakes

6. What do Kool and the Gang want to have a *Celebration* for?
   a. passing the twelfth grade
   b. good times
   c. having found you

7. According to Daryl Hall and John Oates, what can the *Rich Girl* rely on?
   a. the old man's money
   b. all her money-loving friends
   c. their love

8. In *My House*, what will Mary Jane Girls do?
   a. satisfy every fantasy you think of
   b. quench their appetite
   c. make you proud of them

9. What news *Cuts Like a Knife* for Bryan Adams?
   a. he's wanted for loving you
   b. you're somebody else's wife
   c. you might have found somebody new

10. In *Run Away,* how much does Jefferson Starship love you?
    a. as if you were their own
    b. like a son
    c. as much as they would a refugee

11. Foreigner says that you're playing *Head Games* because you won't do what?
    a. show how you feel
    b. give them any tail
    c. leave your other lover

12. In *Take It on the Run,* what did REO Speedwagon hear from a friend of a friend of a friend?
    a. you've got a lot of friends
    b. you've been messing around
    c. you're leaving

13. With what does Steely Dan keep their picture of *Peg*?
    a. their steel guitar
    b. her letter
    c. their Jockey shorts

14. In *Go Your Own Way,* what does Fleetwood Mac say isn't the right thing to do?
    a. love you
    b. hold you down
    c. call your mother

15. In *Take It to the Limit,* what do the Eagles say they've always been?
    a. in love with you
    b. a dreamer
    c. speed-freaks

16. In *Brother Louie,* how do the Stories describe Louie?
    a. blacker than black

    b. bluer than blue

    c. whiter than white

17. Jonathan Edwards wants the *Sunshine* to go away because he's not in the mood for ___.

    a. dancing

    b. looking at anything

    c. getting a tan

18. In *Heartbreaker*, what does Pat Benatar compare your love to?

    a. a six-shooter

    b. a mousetrap

    c. a tidal wave

19. Because *You're the Inspiration*, what does Chicago say they'll do after all that you and they have been through together?

    a. be true to you

    b. cherish the times spent together with you

    c. make it up to you

20. In *Joy to the World*, who was a good friend of Three Dog Night?

    a. Lassie

    b. Jeremiah

    c. their mother

21. What can Sugarloaf's *Green-Eyed Lady* soothe?

    a. their toothache with just one kiss

    b. their irritation

    c. every raging wind that comes

22. When does Stephen Stills say you should *Love the One You're With*?

    a. when you can't be with the one you love

    b. when you're at a party

    c. only when she's the girl you love

23. *In the Summertime,* what is Mungo Jerry's philosophy about life?
   a. life is for living
   b. life's a gas
   c. you only really live in the summertime

24. Because *We're an American Band,* what will Grand Funk Railroad help you do?
   a. learn how to dig their sounds
   b. party down
   c. join them

25. While walking down *Ventura Highway,* what is America chewing on?
   a. a piece of grass
   b. gum
   c. a T-bone steak

26. In *Take My Breath Away,* how does Berlin describe the way they watched you turn their way?
   a. they cried as you melted into their world
   b. their life flashed before their eyes
   c. it was like slow motion

27. What does Steve Miller Band claim in *Jungle Love* that lately you've been doing?
   a. hanging out with the animals
   b. living in the jungle
   c. wearing ropes and chains

28. Even though it was *Only in My Dreams,* what word describes how it seemed for Debbie Gibson?
   a. good
   b. frightening
   c. real

29. How does Devo want you to *Whip It?*
   a. into shape

    b. softly

    c. like you really mean it

30. The Knack wonders whether their time with *My Sharona* is destiny or just ___.

    a. a role of the dice

    b. a lucky break

    c. a game in their mind

31. On what night did Prince meet his *Little Red Corvette*?

    a. Saturday

    b. Thursday

    c. Friday

32. In *Brass in Pocket (I'm Special)*, what do the Pretenders want to get from you?

    a. your diary

    b. your attention

    c. a commitment

33. According to Aerosmith in *Janie's Got a Gun*, where did they find her daddy?

    a. underneath the train

    b. hiding in the closet

    c. in Jamaica

34. In *Macho Man*, what does everyone want to do to the Village People?

    a. dance with them

    b. get out of their way

    c. touch their bodies

35. In *Jack and Diane*, John Cougar Mellancamp says that life goes on long after what?

    a. the thrill of living is gone

    b. the children are grown

    c. she's left him for John

36. According to Blue Oyster Cult in *(Don't Fear) The Reaper*, who are together in eternity?

    a. Moe, Larry, and Curly
    b. them and you
    c. Romeo and Juliet

37. In *More Than a Feeling*, who is it that Boston sees walking away?

    a. Marianne
    b. their shadow
    c. Daisy

38. In *Fallin' in Love*, what do Hamilton, Joe Frank, and Reynolds say it seemed like they did just yesterday?

    a. made up with you
    b. made love for the first time
    c. met you

39. In *Here Comes My Girl*, what word do Tom Petty and the Heartbreakers use to describe the town when their girl isn't around?

    a. boring
    b. hopeless
    c. exciting

40. In *Love Grows (Where My Rosemary Goes)*, how does Edison Lighthouse describe Rosemary's hair?

    a. short and sexy
    b. wild and free
    c. dirty and matted

41. How was the Nitty Gritty Dirt Band's *Mr. Bojangles* dressed?

    a. in worn-out shoes and baggy pants
    b. in gold chains and blue suit
    c. in T-shirt and blue jeans

42. In *My Baby Loves Lovin'*, White Plains says their girlfriend has got what it takes and she knows how to ___.
    a. wear it
    b. dance
    c. use it

43. In *Cum On Feel the Noize*, even though you think their singing is out of time, what does Quiet Riot say about it?
    a. it makes their baby sing
    b. it makes them money
    c. it's got a catchy tune

44. In *Drive*, what do the Cars say you can't go on thinking?
    a. nothing's wrong
    b. living is free
    c. they love someone else

45. In *Carry On Wayward Son*, what does Kansas say will happen in the end?
    a. there'll be peace
    b. you'll return
    c. no one will be left

46. In *Lick It Up*, what doesn't Kiss want you to do until you get to know them better?
    a. share your life with another man
    b. run away
    c. cook

47. In what kind of *Vehicle* does the Ides Of March claim to be a friendly stranger?
    a. a red Mustang
    b. a black sedan
    c. a pink three-window coupe

48. When does Norman Greenbaum plan to go up to the *Spirit in the Sky?*
   a. when he falls in love
   b. next Monday
   c. when he dies

49. In *Rock Me Gently,* what is it Andy Kim says he had never experienced until he met you?
   a. heartaches
   b. a hunger deep inside
   c. a love like this

50. What does Rick Springfield wish about *Jessie's Girl?*
   a. he could be in her shoes
   b. he had her
   c. she'd leave him alone

QUIZ B

1. When does Bon Jovi say you should *Raise Your Hands?*
   a. when it's your turn to speak out
   b. when you want to let a feeling show
   c. when wars have made the silence shake

2. In *Beth,* what does Kiss say they'll be doing all night long?
   a. making love to her
   b. wishing she'd return
   c. playing cards with the boys

3. In *Every Little Thing She Does Is Magic,* even though their life is full of tragic events, what do the Police say about their love for her?
   a. it goes on
   b. it's a mystery
   c. it's the biggest tragedy of all

4. Where is Eddie Money keeping his *Two Tickets to Paradise?*
   a. in his pocket
   b. in a bank vault
   c. with the key to all his dreams

5. Because they're suffering from a *Manic Monday,* what do the Bangles wish for?
   a. Friday
   b. Sunday
   c. a new drug

6. What do the Red Hot Chili Peppers sometimes think is their only friend as they stand *Under the Bridge?*
   a. death
   b. the waters beneath their feet
   c. the city they live in

7. According to Three Dog Night in *Black and White,* what do the children grow up to see?
   a. the light
   b. poverty and prejudice
   c. their dreams come true

8. In *Sweet Child o' Mine,* what do Guns N' Roses say her smile reminds them of?
   a. the sun
   b. childhood memories
   c. wicked things they used to dream about

9. What does *Mickey* do to Toni Basil?
   a. he blows her mind
   b. he puts her down in front of all the guys
   c. he makes the sweetest love to her

10. According to Styx, where are the parts for *Mr. Roboto* made?
    a. in Japan

    b. in a toy factory

    c. in Detroit

11. In *Rock'n Me*, what seems to be getting harder every day for the Steve Miller Band to do?

    a. keep the faith

    b. find a job

    c. keep your love

12. In *When Doves Cry*, in what way is it that Prince thinks you may be just like his mother?

    a. you're both never satisfied

    b. you're both close to his heart

    c. you're both peaceful

13. In *Jump*, what does Van Halen say you've got to do?

    a. swim against the tide

    b. roll with the punches

    c. keep your feet on the ground

14. What does America say the *Tin Man* got from Oz?

    a. nothing that he didn't already have

    b. a heart

    c. an incurable tan

15. Huey Lewis and the News say that *If This Is It*, what should you do?

    a. love them tonight

    b. get to the hospital quickly

    c. let them know

16. In *Come Go With Me*, why does Expose complain about your coming home?

    a. they don't want to see you again

    b. you're never alone

    c. you come home late

17. In *I Can't Go for That (No Can Do)*, what do Daryl Hall and John Oates say they'll do for you?

    a. be your friend, but nothing more
    b. almost anything you want them to
    c. help you move out

18. In *How Much I Feel,* what does Ambrosia say they still see when they make love to their wife at night?
    a. their past flashing before their eyes
    b. your face
    c. spots before their eyes

19. According to Three Dog Night, where is *An Old Fashioned Love Song* playing?
    a. on the radio
    b. in their mind
    c. in lovers' hearts

20. What do Alive and Kicking want you to do *Tighter, Tighter?*
    a. save money
    b. make love to them
    c. hold on

21. What does Carlos Santana say the *Black Magic Woman* is trying to do to him?
    a. help him get back with his lady
    b. put a spell of love over him
    c. make a devil out of him

22. In *It's So Nice to Be With You,* Gallery says it's so nice to hear you say ___.
    a. their name
    b. you're going to please them
    c. anything that's on your mind

23. Although the *Magic Man* told Heart that they didn't have to love him, what did he want to do?
    a. get high awhile
    b. take a chance
    c. make them beg

24. According to Lisa Lisa and Cult Jam in *Head to Toe*, what did today start off with?
    a. a phone call from you
    b. an argument
    c. a crazy kiss

25. According to the Motels, what is it that *Only the Lonely* can do?
    a. play
    b. cry
    c. understand how they feel

26. In *Sharing the Night Together*, what does Dr. Hook ask if you'd like?
    a. a Tootsie Roll
    b. to slip away into the night
    c. someone new to talk to

27. In *Love in an Elevator*, what does Aerosmith say they're going to have?
    a. a fantasy
    b. heart failure
    c. a sweet ride

28. The Bellamy Brothers want you to *Let Your Love Flow* like what?
    a. a cascading waterfall
    b. veins and arteries
    c. a mountain stream

29. What do the Beach Boys say about *Kokomo*?
    a. it's got no surf
    b. it's a place to get away from it all
    c. it's just a state of mind

30. According to the Atlanta Rhythm Section, what does an *Imaginary Lover* never do?
    a. cheat on you
    b. knock at your door
    c. turn you down

31. What does Fleetwood Mac call *Sara*?
    a. the poet in their heart
    b. the biggest pain in their side
    c. their angel from heaven

32. Why does Soul Asylum say they are a *Runaway Train* never going back?
    a. they've heard too many lies
    b. it's easier than dealing with the pain
    c. the future beyond is brighter

33. In what color is Nick Gilder's *Hot Child in the City* dressed?
    a. fluorescent green
    b. shocking pink
    c. black

34. In *Hangin' Tough*, what do the New Kids on the Block dare you to do if you want to take a chance?
    a. go out with them
    b. strip down to your boxers
    c. do the New Kids dance

35. In *Two Out of Three Ain't Bad*, what does Meat Loaf say about talking all night?
    a. that isn't going to get them anywhere
    b. it'll lead them to the truth
    c. it's a good way to stay awake

36. What does Lighthouse hope one day to be doing with the *Pretty Lady*?
    a. dressing her as a pretty man
    b. raising a family
    c. making love to her

37. Where does the Ozark Mountain Daredevil's *Jackie Blue* live her life?
    a. inside a room
    b. up in the mountains
    c. in her mind

38. In *Dance With Me*, what does Orleans want you to be?

   a. homecoming queen
   b. their partner
   c. more friendly

39. According to Player in *Baby Come Back*, who can the blame be put on?

   a. nobody
   b. them
   c. jealous friends

40. At the *Y.M.C.A.*, the Village People say you can find many ways to ___.

   a. fall in love
   b. lose your pride
   c. have a good time

41. In *Fly Like an Eagle*, what does the Steve Miller Band say about time?

   a. it keeps slipping into the future
   b. tomorrow's never the same as yesterday
   c. it's too late to turn back now

42. In *Renegade*, who does Styx say is coming down to greet them?

   a. their baby
   b. the grim reaper
   c. the hangman

43. According to Bonnie Tyler in *It's a Heartache*, you'll love until what breaks?

   a. your arms
   b. your heart
   c. your pride

44. How and when does Blondie say you can *Call Me*?

   a. in your dreams, at night
   b. on the line, anytime
   c. loud and clear, now

45. Where could R.E.M. be found *Losing My Religion*?
    a. on the church steps
    b. in the spotlight
    c. in your arms

46. According to Pat Benatar in *Hell Is for Children*, why do the children cry in the dark?
    a. someone turned out the lights
    b. they are alone
    c. so you can't see their tears

47. Why does Toto say to *Hold the Line*?
    a. because sometimes love's a crime
    b. because love isn't always on time
    c. because hanging up is a bad sign

48. Bread wonders *If* a picture paints a thousands words, ___.
    a. then why can't they paint you
    b. then why are you so blue
    c. then why can't a blind man dream

49. What does Corey Hart do with his *Sunglasses at Night*?
    a. he puts them under his pillow
    b. he wears them
    c. he hides them in the drawer

50. In *One*, what does Metallica say is the only thing that is real for them now?
    a. pain
    b. your love
    c. their own life

BONUS QUIZ

1. What does Climax consider to be *Precious and Few?*
   a. your love
   b. their friends
   c. the moments they share with you

2. In *Do You Know What I Mean*, who was stepping out with Lee Michael's girlfriend?
   a. Bobby
   b. Tommy
   c. Sally

3. What is Heart listening to *Alone?*
   a. the beating of their heart
   b. the empty silence
   c. the ticking of the clock

4. Journey is waiting with *Open Arms*, wondering what?
   a. how they could have let you so down
   b. why no one else is around
   c. who will answer their prayers

5. In *I've Found Someone of My Own*, what did Free Movement's mate tell them she had found?
   a. somebody to take their place
   b. a new place to stay
   c. true love

6. When the Five Man Electrical Band read one of the *Signs* that said "long-haired freaky people need not apply" and went in to see why, what did they say sarcastically when the employer said "I think you'll do"?

    a. Yeah, but do what?!
    b. Imagine that, me working for you!
    c. Shows you how stupid you are!

7. In *Still the Same,* what was the trick you told Bob Seger and the Silver Bullet Band?
    a. never play the same cards twice
    b. get out when the going's rough
    c. never play the game too long

8. In *Do It Again,* although you hide the cards when gambling, what does Steely Dan say you must do in Las Vegas, the land of milk and honey?
    a. lay them on the table
    b. back them up with money
    c. go for broke

9. How does Bruce Springsteen describe the town in which he was *Born in the USA?*
    a. as a country place
    b. as a dead-man's town
    c. as the only place to be born

10. At the *Dead Man's Party,* what does Oingo Boingo ask you to leave at the front door?
    a. all your worries and cares
    b. your shoes
    c. your body

11. Who is telling the story of *The Night They Drove Old Dixie Down* according to Joan Baez?
    a. Virgil Caine
    b. Boxcar Willie
    c. Robert E. Lee

12. According to Deep Purple in *Smoke on the Water,* who had the best place around until someone burned it to the ground?

    a. they did
    b. Frank Zappa and the Mothers
    c. The Queen of England

13. What does Pearl Jam say *Jeremy* did in class today?
    a. he made a pass at the teacher
    b. he stole some money
    c. he spoke

14. Where are Brewer and Shipley sitting while they're *One Toke Over the Line?*
    a. on the dock of the bay
    b. in a railway station
    c. in jail

15. According to Reunion in *Life Is a Rock*, what is at the end of the rainbow?
    a. the greatest band that ever lived
    b. the answer to your dreams
    c. a golden oldie

16. According to Steely Dan in *Deacon Blue*, what is this the night of?
    a. new hopes and dreams
    b. the expanding man
    c. winners and losers

17. In *Gloria*, what does Laura Branigan say you're headed for?
    a. a breakdown
    b. stardom
    c. a new kind of high

18. According to Skid Row, what is the name of the boy who's facing *18 and Life?*
    a. Toby
    b. Spanky
    c. Ricky

19. In *Authority Song*, what does John Cougar Mellen-camp say about authority?
    a. it's a necessary evil in the world
    b. it always wins
    c. we don't have to take it

20. What does *Wall of Voodoo* hear, though barely understand, being discussed on the Mexican Radio?
    a. foreign immigration
    b. Western inflation
    c. drugs

UK Contemporary Rock
(1970s-1990s)

UK contemporary rock encompasses all the stars from abroad who have given us rock and roll sounds in the days that have followed the original British Invasion; from early favorites such as the Police, Air Supply, and Dire Straits up through present hot rockers like Genesis, Peter Gabriel, and UB40.

QUIZ A

1. When rock was young in *Crocodile Rock*, Elton John had so much fun in his old gold ___.
   a. Benz
   b. Chevy
   c. woody

2. According to Shocking Blue, *Venus* wants to be your ___.
   a. fire
   b. shining star
   c. dream machine

3. The Rolling Stones say that if you *Start Me Up*, what will they do?
   a. walk away
   b. crank you up
   c. never stop

4. What do the Police say they'll be doing with *Every Breath You Take?*
   - a. capturing it in their mouth
   - b. analyzing its alcohol level
   - c. watching you

5. What does Genesis say happens when the girl with the *Invisible Touch* crawls under your skin?
   - a. you've got an urge to scratch
   - b. love will soon bite
   - c. you're never quite the same

6. How old is Abba's *Dancing Queen?*
   - a. sixteen
   - b. seventeen
   - c. forty-three

7. What does the Electric Light Orchestra say they've got to do with their *Sweet Talkin' Woman?*
   - a. get back to her
   - b. tame her down
   - c. keep listening to her sweet lies

8. In *Sledgehammer,* if you call Peter Gabriel, what will he be for you?
   - a. your screw
   - b. your microphone
   - c. anything you need

9. In *White Wedding,* what does Billy Idol say it's a nice day to do?
   - a. get married
   - b. start again
   - c. dye your hair white

10. In *Reminiscing,* what band was Little River Band listening to while they held your hand?
    - a. the Beatles
    - b. Glenn Miller
    - c. Roger Williams

11. According to Led Zeppelin in *Stairway to Heaven*, what does the lady who is there show everyone?
    a. she's not wearing underwear
    b. dreams really can come true
    c. all that glitters is gold

12. According to the Alan Parsons Project in *Games People Play*, when do people mostly play these games?
    a. on the weekends
    b. on a Saturday night
    c. in the middle of the night

13. In *All Out of Love*, what does Air Supply say they can't be too late in saying?
    a. they were wrong
    b. they love you
    c. goodbye

14. In *Head Over Heels*, what does Tears For Fears want to talk about alone with you?
    a. their future
    b. the weather
    c. whatever's on your mind

15. What is it that Milli Vanilli claims *Girl You Know It's True*?
    a. you've been messing around
    b. they really can sing
    c. they love you

16. In *Here I Am*, what comes crashing through for Air Supply?
    a. reality
    b. memories
    c. heartache

17. In *Imagine*, what does John Lennon say you might call him?
    a. Mr. Lennon

    b. a dreamer

    c. the walrus

18. What does Badfinger give *Day After Day* to you?

    a. their love

    b. promises they can't keep

    c. new hope

19. What do the Police say *Roxanne* doesn't have to do?

    a. apologize

    b. live a double life

    c. turn on her red light

20. Rod Stewart would find a *Reason to Believe* if he did what?

    a. listened long enough to you

    b. listened to what his friends told him

    c. forgot what you said the night before

21. In *Another Brick in the Wall*, what does Pink Floyd ask the teachers to do?

    a. listen to their song

    b. leave the kids alone

    c. make learning fun

22. What does Air Supply want to do in their *Sweet Dreams*?

    a. ride the skies

    b. make sweet love to you

    c. never wake up

23. In *Alone Again (Naturally)*, what does Gilbert O'Sullivan intend to do after he climbs to the top of the tower?

    a. gaze at the people below

    b. jump off

    c. daydream

24. In *One More Night*, what has Phil Collins been trying to let you know for so long?

a. that he can stay with you only for tonight
b. that he needs his freedom
c. how he feels

25. The Alan Parsons Project is the *Eye in the Sky* and also the maker of ___.
a. dreams
b. fools
c. tears

26. Wham! wants you to *Wake Me Up Before You Go-Go* so they can do what tonight?
a. dance
b. make love to you
c. go back to sleep

27. Although Eric Clapton says *I Shot the Sheriff,* what does he say he didn't do?
a. shoot the deputy
b. lock him up
c. run from the law

28. In *More Than I Can Say,* what does Leo Sayer say he'll do tomorrow?
a. things he forgot to do today
b. love you twice as much
c. tell you how he feels

29. In *Karma Chameleon,* Culture Club says that they're your lover, not your ___.
a. rival
b. brother
c. candy man

30. Because he's got a *Bad Case of Loving You,* what does Robert Palmer say won't cure him?
a. a cold shower
b. a pill
c. anything less than your sweet kiss

31. Although INXS says they *Need You Tonight*, what do they say about your moves?
    a. they're totally unpredictable
    b. they're making them want you now
    c. they're so raw

32. In *Take on Me*, when does A-ha say they'll be gone?
    a. in a day or two
    b. the next time you leave them alone
    c. when the stars no longer shine

33. According to Dire Straits in *Money for Nothing*, what is it you want for free?
    a. lunch
    b. respect
    c. chicks

34. What does Billy Idol say they cry at midnight as their *Rebel Yell*?
    a. more, more, more
    b. burn, baby, burn
    c. give 'em hell

35. According to Duran Duran, where does *Rio* dance?
    a. in the disco
    b. in their dreams
    c. on the sand

36. In *Hold Me Now*, how do the Thompson Twins describe their life with you now?
    a. tattered and torn
    b. fresh and alive
    c. tight

37. What do others think about the way the Rolling Stones are acting because they *Miss You*?
    a. people think they're really in love
    b. people think they're crazy
    c. people avoid them on the streets

38. What is the problem George Harrison has in meeting *My Sweet Lord?*

    a. he doesn't know where to look

    b. he doesn't know what to ask

    c. it takes so long

39. According to the Eurythmics in *Sweet Dreams (Are Made of This),* although some people want to use you, what do other people prefer?

    a. to be abused

    b. to run away

    c. to drink their own life away

40. Because they were *Lost in Love,* what did Air Supply find out that they needed?

    a. a cure for their disease

    b. someone to show them

    c. a prayer

41. Rod Stewart says that *Hot Legs* can make love to him tonight, but what does he want her to do tomorrow?

    a. make love again

    b. go dancing with him

    c. be gone

42. Before *You Made Me Believe in Magic,* what did the Bay City Rollers think about their life?

    a. that it was upside down

    b. that it never changed

    c. that love would always pass them by

43. What does Wings have to say about what others call *Silly Love Songs?*

    a. they sure sell a lot of records

    b. there's nothing silly about love

    c. what's wrong with that?

44. According to UB40 in *Can't Help Falling in Love*, what do wise men say?

   a. love conquers all
   b. love makes for a strange bedfellow
   c. only fools rush in

45. In *Freedom*, what does George Michael say about clothes?

   a. they can turn a clown into a prince
   b. sometimes they don't make the man
   c. it's nice to wear as little as possible

46. What is it you don't do that makes Adam Ant call you a *Goody Two Shoes*?

   a. drink or smoke
   b. kiss him goodnight
   c. go the distance

47. According to Men At Work in *Down Under*, what did the lady who made them nervous do for them?

   a. she made them a vegemite sandwich
   b. she gave them breakfast
   c. she put them in their place

48. Even though *People Are People*, what does Depeche Mode wonder?

   a. why they can't say what's really on their minds
   b. why you and they should get along so awfully
   c. whether there will ever be peace in the world

49. According to Paul McCartney in *Another Day*, where does the lady await the man of her dreams who might break her loneliness spell?

   a. in the street
   b. outside a bar
   c. in her apartment

50. What is Bananarama trying to do in *Cruel Summer* even though the air is so heavy and dry?

a. smile
b. fly
c. pretend you still care

QUIZ B

1. According to Elton John, what is going to catch you when *The Bitch Is Back?*
   a. her love
   b. the fever
   c. the truth

2. In *Fernando*, if they had the chance to do it all again, what does Abba say they'd do?
   a. run like the wind
   b. ask you to change your name
   c. the same thing

3. In *Careless Whisper*, what does Wham! now realize they should have known better than to do?
   a. whisper that they love you
   b. cheat a friend
   c. take your sister along

4. Although Rod Stewart knows he is keeping his *Maggie May* happy, what does he also fear?
   a. soon he'll be sued
   b. she'll soon be too old for him
   c. he's being used

5. What can Peter Gabriel see *In Your Eyes?*
   a. his reflection
   b. pain
   c. love

6. In *Who Can It Be Now*, what is it that Men At Work wish?
   a. to be left alone

    b. for you to care

    c. to be able to change the past

7. According to Bananarama, how did *Venus* appear?

    a. like the eighth wonder of the world

    b. in a Ninja Turtle disguise

    c. black as the dark night

8. In *Don't Bring Me Down*, what does the Electric Light Orchestra say you want to do?

    a. go out with your fancy friends

    b. get married

    c. make them feel that they're the guilty ones

9. Because he has a *Groovy Kind of Love*, what does Phil Collins have to do to stop from being blue?

    a. dance to the rhythm of your beat

    b. make love to you

    c. look at you

10. In *Isn't It Time*, what was the last thing the Babys had on their mind?

    a. leaving you behind

    b. falling in love

    c. calling you on the phone

11. In *King of Pain*, where do the Police say there's a little black spot?

    a. in their heart

    b. on their lungs

    c. on the sun

12. What is Duran Duran's *Hungry Like the Wolf* trying to do?

    a. hunt for you

    b. quench their appetite for love

    c. get a meal

13. What does the First Class want their *Beach Baby* to give them?

a. something they can remember her by
b. sugar and spice
c. her love and devotion

14. In *Long Cool Woman (in a Black Dress)*, what night were the Hollies downtown, working on a case?
a. Tuesday
b. Friday
c. Saturday

15. Although Phil Collins says *Sussudio* likes him, what does he add?
a. he never met a girl with a name like hers
b. she likes everyone she's ever met
c. she doesn't know his name

16. In *Help Is on Its Way*, what does the Little River Band say you should do if you're always in confusion?
a. sort it out
b. call on them
c. believe in rock and roll

17. Why does Badfinger say to *Come and Get It* quickly?
a. they can't wait forever
b. it's getting cold
c. it may not last

18. In *Instant Karma (We All Shine On)*, John Lennon says you'd better get yourself together and ___.
a. join the human race
b. go to church
c. make the world all right

19. According to Duran Duran in *Too Much Information*, even though the band is perfect, what shouldn't you do?
a. expect them to stay that way forever

    b. scratch the surface

    c. criticize them

20. According to the Elton John Band in *Philadelphia Freedom*, what did Elton used to be if the cause was right?

    a. the bell of freedom

    b. a piano man

    c. a rolling stone

21. How does *Red Red Wine* make UB40 feel?

    a. fine

    b. drunk

    c. thirsty for more

22. What does the Little River Band want to do with their *Lady*?

    a. take her on a trip aboard their ship

    b. take a look at her

    c. make love to her

23. In *Head First*, what are the Babys and their girl doing tonight?

    a. giving birth

    b. going out

    c. making love

24. According to Iron Maiden, what is *The Number of the Beast*?

    a. 666

    b. 13

    c. 1999

25. According to David Bowie in *Space Oddity*, what is the name of the astronaut?

    a. Captain Kirk

    b. Major Thom

    c. Sergeant Lowe

26. In *Photograph*, what does Def Leppard say you make every man feel like?
    a. a child
    b. a fool
    c. a movie star

27. In *Hooked on a Feeling*, what is Blue Swede high on believing?
    a. that you're in love with them
    b. that you're their lucky star
    c. that it's not what you say, but how much you mean it

28. Where are the Rolling Stones standing, *Waiting on a Friend*?
    a. near a phone booth
    b. at your front porch
    c. in a doorway

29. What does Iron Maiden seek *Sanctuary* from?
    a. the pitiless souls
    b. a world of make believe
    c. the law

30. In *Every Woman in the World*, although Air Supply was partying every night, what didn't they know?
    a. that they were not alone
    b. what happiness really meant
    c. that you would never come

31. In *Do You Think I'm Sexy*, what does Rod Stewart ask you to do if you really want him?
    a. let him know
    b. tell your other friend to leave
    c. ask your other friends to come

32. Why does Phil Collins want you to *Take Me Home*?
    a. it's cold outside

    b. he's been drinking again

    c. because he can't remember

33. While talking about the *Tiger in a Spotlight*, what do Emerson, Lake, and Palmer ask?

    a. Is their love tough enough for you?

    b. Have you ever wondered why?

    c. Can they be your tiger for a night?

34. What didn't John Lennon mean to cause his *Woman*?

    a. a reason to doubt him

    b. sorrow and pain

    c. sleepless nights

35. In *Daniel*, what country does Elton John see the red taillights of the plane heading for?

    a. America

    b. Mexico

    c. Spain

36. In *Ring Around Your Finger*, what have the Police come seeking?

    a. your hand in marriage

    b. the names of all your other lovers

    c. knowledge

37. In *Tears in Heaven*, what does Eric Clapton wonder would happen if he saw you up in heaven?

    a. would you speak to him

    b. would you know his name

    c. could he move in with you

38. What will Metal Church do like a *Ton of Bricks*?

    a. defend you

    b. blow the place apart

    c. hit you

39. In *Comfortably Numb*, what did Pink Floyd say their hands felt like when they were children and had the fever?
   a. balloons
   b. pillows
   c. hot metal anvils

40. Where does Duran Duran see *Girls on Film* walking hand in hand at midnight?
   a. across the bridge
   b. on the stage
   c. along the beach

41. According to Thin Lizzy, what caused the *Suicide*?
   a. a hit single
   b. a love gone sour
   c. a bullet

42. What do the Rolling Stones tell *Angie?*
   a. no one can say they didn't try
   b. she's the girl they've always dreamed of
   c. they're free to do whatever they want any old time

43. In *The One That You Love*, what doesn't Air Supply want you to tell them?
   a. that the morning has come so soon
   b. that they are not the one
   c. where you want to be touched

44. Because *Tonight's the Night (Gonna Be Alright)*, what does Rod Stewart want his angel to do?
   a. fly away
   b. make his night shine
   c. spread her wings

45. Who does Phil Collins ask *Don't Lose My Number?*
   a. Rikki
   b. Billy
   c. Betty

46. Although Elton John feels *Your Song* is simple, he hopes you don't mind that he wrote down how wonderful life is while ___.
   a. you're in the world
   b. he's all alone
   c. you're in love with him

47. According to the Babys, *If You've Got the Time,* what do they have?
   a. the way to make things better
   b. the beer
   c. the love

48. According to U2, what happened on April 4 for *Pride (in the Name of Love)?*
   a. someone was shot
   b. they fell in love for the first time
   c. man landed on the moon

49. In *Rock of Ages,* what does Def Leppard want to do?
   a. stand up and be strong
   b. rock the place to the ground
   c. find the true meaning of love

50. On what does U2 say she makes them wait *With or Without You?*
   a. faith and hope
   b. a bed of nails
   c. pins and needles

BONUS QUIZ

1. Where is the club in which the Kinks met *Lola*?
   a. in Paris
   b. in Soho
   c. in Greenwich Village

2. In *Silent Lucidity*, Queensryche asks if the dream is over or whether ___.
   a. there was ever a dream at all
   b. it has just begun
   c. it was all for real

3. According to George Michael in *I Want Your Sex*, if you look into his eyes what won't you need?
   a. a Bible
   b. anymore dreams
   c. a reason

4. In *Break My Stride*, how does Matthew Wilder say he dreamed he went to find you in China?
   a. by row boat
   b. in his yacht
   c. on the wings of love

5. In *Owner of a Lonely Heart*, what does Yes say you always live your life without doing?
   a. talking it over with them
   b. giving everyone else an even break
   c. thinking of the future

6. According to Ozzy Osbourne, what was the *Iron Man* turned into in a magnetic field?
   a. a heap of scrap
   b. steel
   c. the Iron Woman

7. According to King Crimson, what has just begun in *The Court of the Crimson King*?
   a. the play
   b. the magic act
   c. the tournament

8. In *Run to the Hills*, what did Iron Maiden do on the plains?
   a. they made love to you
   b. they fought the Redskins
   c. they ran away from the world

9. According to Dire Straits in *Sultans of Swing*, why doesn't Harry mind if he makes the scene or not?
   a. because he's got a girl waiting for him at home
   b. because he's not a fan of the music
   c. because he's got a daytime job

10. According to Thin Lizzy in *The Boys Are Back in Town*, what did a girl do at Johnny's party?
    a. she slapped Johnny's face
    b. she danced for all the guys
    c. she took Johnny upstairs

11. During those *Dance Hall Days*, what does Wang Chung say everyone was cool on?
    a. making free love
    b. Christ
    c. Coke and Pepsi

12. In *Neanderthal Man*, what does Hotlegs want to do with you?
    a. make Neanderthal love
    b. escape to their own world
    c. carry you to their cave

13. Because they're the *Sinner*, what doesn't Judas Priest have to do?
    a. say they're sorry

    b. tell the truth

    c. fall to their knees and pray

14. How long have the Animals felt the chill of *The Night?*

    a. since the sun went down

    b. for a week or so

    c. ever since she's been gone

15. In *Making Love Out of Nothing At All,* although Air Supply knows how to do almost anything, what didn't they know at all?

    a. how to get close to you

    b. how to make you notice them

    c. how to leave you

16. In *I Was Only Joking,* what does Rod Stewart lament doing?

    a. being a fool for you

    b. pouring out his heart for prosperity

    c. making you fall in love when he wasn't really serious

17. In *Save a Prayer,* where does Duran Duran say the lights are flashing?

    a. on the ceiling

    b. on your window sill

    c. in their heart

18. What does Sting say you can do, though you'll still know *Nothin' 'Bout Me?*

    a. run every test from A to Z

    b. build him up or put him down

    c. make love to him when you want

19. What do Emerson, Lake, and Palmer say the *Lucky Man* had?

    a. magic dice

    b. a lovin' wife

    c. horses and women

20. Where does Dio say the *Holy Diver* has been down too long?
     a.   in the midnight sea
     b.   in the river of Jordan
     c.   in your ocean

Easy Listening
(1950s-1990s)

Easy listening, though not exactly rock and roll, has always been closely connected to it, from the early songs of Johnny Mathis and the Platters to the more recent successes of Kenny Rogers and Linda Ronstadt. The music has always been unabashedly simple—almost naive—unpretentious, and without an "attitude." Maybe that's why stars such as Barbra Streisand and Anne Murray are always just a song away from returning to the spotlight; as the category implies, it's easy to do because . . . after all, it's easy listening.

QUIZ A

1. The Vogues want you to *Turn Around, Look at Me*, to see ___.
   a. their tears
   b. who really loves you
   c. what you've left behind

2. Why do the Happenings have to wait in *See You in September*?
   a. because of summer vacation
   b. you're moving away
   c. you don't want to see them until September

3. What is Seals and Crofts' *Summer Breeze* blowing through?
   a. their memory
   b. the jasmine
   c. their T-shirt

4. Why is it the Serendipity Singers plead *Don't Let the Rain Come Down?*
   a. they want to cry alone
   b. they're not insured
   c. their roof has a hole in it

5. What does Pat Boone ask you to do in *Don't Forbid Me?*
   a. see other girls
   b. hold you tight
   c. tie you down

6. What is Connie Francis's dream about *Where the Boys Are?*
   a. that someone waits for her
   b. to get married
   c. to have one boy on each arm

7. What is the only reason the Carpenters can find to explain why they are on *Top of the World?*
   a. they've climbed the ladder of love
   b. it's because you're around
   c. they took the right off-ramp

8. In *Never Be the Same*, what does Christopher Cross say sometimes slips out of sight?
   a. love
   b. the truth
   c. the ship of dreams

9. In *Sometimes When We Touch*, why does Dan Hill choke on his reply when you ask him if he loves you?

   a. he thinks it's a stupid question
   b. he never thought you'd ever ask him how he feels
   c. he'd rather hurt you honestly than mislead you with a lie

10. According to Walter Egan, who are the *Magnet and Steel?*
   a. his parents
   b. you are the magnet, he is steel
   c. the angel of love is the magnet, you are steel

11. In *It Might Be You,* where is Stephen Bishop lying, wishing there would be someone waiting at home for him?
   a. on his bed
   b. in a cloud of hope
   c. on the sand

12. According to Diana Ross and Lionel Richie in *Endless Love,* what do your eyes tell them?
   a. that you've been up all night
   b. how much you care
   c. that love has no limits

13. In *My Angel Baby,* what can Toby Beau read between the lines?
   a. you're too good to be true
   b. you've got leaving on your mind
   c. you're the devil in disguise

14. According to Roberta Flack and Donny Hathaway, *The Closer I Get to You* what happens?
   a. the more you make them see
   b. the more you turn away
   c. the more they fall in love

15. What does Dan Fogelberg say he's done *Longer* than there've been stars in the heavens?

   a. he's been in love with you
   b. he's been waiting for you
   c. he's been hoping for an answer

16. In *Feelings*, what is Morris Albert trying to do?
   a. understand what love is
   b. forget her
   c. walk again

17. In *Too Much, Too Little, Too Late*, what did Johnny Mathis and Deniece Williams know would have to happen one day?
   a. they'd have to open separate bank accounts
   b. they'd have to explain to their parents why they came home late
   c. their love would end this way

18. According to Paul Davis, when is it that *I Go Crazy?*
   a. when he looks in your eyes
   b. when you whisper softly in his ear
   c. whenever he hears his favorite song

19. What turns Dorothy Moore's whole life *Misty Blue?*
   a. your goodbye
   b. a blueberry shower
   c. the thought of you

20. According to Don Ho, where can *Tiny Bubbles* be found?
   a. in the wine
   b. on the moon
   c. in your eyes

21. According to Frank Sinatra, what do *Love and Marriage* go together like?
   a. a bed and breakfast
   b. a horse and carriage
   c. bag and baggage

22. In *You're No Good*, how does Linda Ronstadt feel now that you and she are through?
    a. helpless
    b. sadder but wiser
    c. better

23. What would Peaches and Herb do *For Your Love*?
    a. rob, cheat, and kill
    b. anything
    c. slash their wrists

24. According to Captain and Tennille in *Muskrat Love*, what are Susie and Sam doing in Muskrat land?
    a. dancing to the jitterbug
    b. playing games
    c. getting married in the chapel

25. What does Nat "King" Cole say you can't do to a *Ramblin' Rose*?
    a. cling to it
    b. get stuck
    c. ever say goodbye

26. Firefall reminds you to *Just Remember I Love You* when ___.
    a. the going gets rough
    b. you go to bed at night
    c. the thrill is gone

27. According to Spandau Ballet, what is *True*?
    a. everything that isn't false
    b. their love
    c. the words they've spoken tonight

28. In *You Light Up My Life*, what do you give to Debby Boone?
    a. the stars in the sky
    b. a cigarette and a smile
    c. hope to carry on

29. What are the Four Lads *Standing on the* Corner doing?
    a. watching all the girls go by
    b. casing the neighborhood
    c. leaning on a lamppost

30. Why does Kenny Nolan say *I Like Dreamin'*?
    a. because the real world makes him blue
    b. because dreamin' will make you his
    c. because that's when he can do his schemin'

31. In *The Gambler*, what does Kenny Rogers say you should never do while you're sitting at the table?
    a. drop the cards on the floor
    b. look at the dealer's eyes
    c. count your money

32. According to Tony Bennett in *I Left My Heart in San Francisco*, what special attractions climb halfway to the stars?
    a. the Nob Hill bars
    b. the cable cars
    c. the houses from afar

33. For Marvin Gaye and Tammi Terrell, with every passing minute of *Your Precious Love*, what is wrapped up in their life?
    a. another memory
    b. another minute wasted
    c. joy

34. In *To Know Him Is to Love Him*, what do the Teddy Bears' friends say will happen?
    a. he'll leave them one day alone and broken-hearted
    b. their love will continue to grow until eternity
    c. there will come a day when they'll walk alongside of him

35. What is Glen Cambell, the *Rhinestone Cowboy,* getting from people he doesn't even know?

 a. letters
 b. complaints
 c. marriage proposals

36. In *I Love How You Love Me,* what is it you do that thrills the Paris Sisters every time you kiss them?

 a. you tickle them in their favorite place
 b. you close your eyes
 c. you hiccup

37. According to Mercy, *Love (Can Make You Happy)* when your mind is filled with thoughts of ___.

 a. another boy
 b. someone you love
 c. the Lord

38. In *Fire and Rain,* when was James Taylor told that his woman had left?

 a. an hour ago
 b. yesterday morning
 c. last night

39. According to the Carpenters, *It's Going to Take Some Time* to do what?

 a. make up
 b. find a new love
 c. get in shape

40. In *Since I Fell For You,* Lenny Welch cautions that when you give love but never get love in return, then you had best ___.

 a. let love depart
 b. keep trying until love succeeds
 c. take a better look at love

41. According to Astrud Gilberto, when *The Girl From Ipanema* walks to the sea, where are her eyes focused?
    a. toward the clouds
    b. on the boys' private parts
    c. straight ahead

42. According to Debbie Reynolds, what is so special now in the life of *Tammy*?
    a. she's pregnant
    b. she's sixteen
    c. she's in love

43. In *Easy*, what do the Commodores say they're doing tomorrow?
    a. leaving
    b. planning to see you
    c. going to the prom with you

44. In *Go Away Little Girl*, why does Steve Lawrence say he's not supposed to be with you?
    a. he belongs to someone else
    b. you're too young to be seen with him
    c. you make him stutter and sneeze

45. When Glen Campbell left *Galveston*, how old was the girl he left behind?
    a. sixteen
    b. twenty-one
    c. eight

46. What place is waiting *26 Miles* across the sea for the Four Preps?
    a. Santa Catalina
    b. Hawaii
    c. the Bahamas

47. In *We'll Sing in the Sunshine*, what did Gale Garnett's father tell her regarding her relationship with a man?

   a. don't just love any man
   b. love him with all your heart
   c. save your heart for the one who cares

48. In *Put a Little Love in Your Heart*, what does Jackie DeShannon hope will be your guide when you look around at the world?
   a. patience
   b. urgency
   c. kindness

49. What is it that you've left the Platters to do all alone in *The Great Pretender*?
   a. dream
   b. start a new life
   c. fall in love

50. The Lettermen say that *When I Fall in Love*, how long will it last?
   a. until eternity
   b. forever
   c. until one and one is three

QUIZ B

1. To what query does Johnny Mathis refer when he replies *Until the Twelfth of Never*?
   a. how long he'll wait for you to return
   b. how long he'll love you
   c. what day precedes the thirteenth of never

2. According to Richard Harris, what did someone leave out in the rain at *MacArthur Park*?
   a. the cake
   b. an umbrella
   c. the picnic basket

3. In *I Got Rhythm*, who won't be found around the Happenings' door?

    a. Old Man Trouble
    b. old girlfriends
    c. adults

4. In *Something Stupid*, what words do Frank and Nancy Sinatra say always spoils the evening?
    a. I love you
    b. give me the bill
    c. it's time to go home

5. In *White on White*, who does Bobby Vinton say is getting married today?
    a. he is
    b. his older sister
    c. his little angel

6. Although Connie Francis knows that *Everybody's Somebody's Fool*, what couldn't she do to escape?
    a. close her eyes
    b. say goodbye
    c. run and hide

7. In *What the World Needs Now Is Love*, Jackie De-Shannon says love isn't just for some but for ___.
    a. everyone
    b. the blessed
    c. you and me

8. According to the Four Aces in *Love Is a Many Splendored Thing*, love is nature's way of giving a reason to be ___.
    a. human
    b. living
    c. hooked on a feeling

9. What does Glen Campbell say his wife will be doing *By the Time I Get to Phoenix*?
    a. cooking breakfast
    b. brushing her teeth
    c. rising

10. In *This Guy's in Love With You*, what has Herb Alpert overheard regarding your feelings for him?
    a. you think he's shy
    b. you think he's weird
    c. you think he's fine

11. The Commodores say it's time to tell you that you've been *Three Times a Lady* now that they've come to the end of what?
    a. the rainbow
    b. their rope
    c. the evening

12. What does Johnny Mathis admit *It's Not for Me to Say* about you?
    a. that you'll always care
    b. how long he'll love you
    c. whether you can see other guys

13. The Caravelles say *You Don't Have to Be a Baby to Cry* or to ___.
    a. dream all day
    b. eat Gerber's food
    c. lie awake all night long

14. In *Jamaica Farewell*, in what city did Harry Belafonte leave a girlfriend behind?
    a. Kingston
    b. Miami
    c. Papeete

15. Because *Love Won't Let Me Wait*, where does Major Harris need you?
    a. back home
    b. next to him
    c. in his pocket, on a chain

16. In *Secret Lovers*, what does Atlantic Starr wish they didn't have to do?
    a. keep their love out of sight

    b. go home alone

    c. make love with their masks on

17. According to Christopher Cross in *Arthur's Theme*, the best that you can do is fall in love when you are caught between what two places?

    a. loneliness and despair

    b. a rock and a hard place

    c. the moon and New York City

18. In what did Bobby Vinton write *Roses Are Red* for his girlfriend during graduation day?

    a. inside her graduation card

    b. in a box containing a wedding ring

    c. in her yearbook

19. What has happened to Crystal Gayle to make her realize *Don't It Make My Brown Eyes Blue?*

    a. her dreams are coming true

    b. you've found someone new

    c. she discovered the magic of contact lenses

20. In *When Will I Be Loved*, what happens every time Linda Ronstadt meets a new love?

    a. he breaks her heart in two

    b. she feels the same electric spark rush through her heart

    c. she adds another notch to her belt

21. Because they're *Together* with you, where could Tierra be even though it wouldn't matter?

    a. on the moon

    b. drowning in the sea of love

    c. lost on a desert

22. Although he doesn't know if he's being foolish or wise, what does John Paul Young say he must do when *Love Is in the Air?*

    a. believe in it

    b. go for it with all his might

    c. smell the roses

23. Although she is here and warm for Bob Welch, what does he say would happen to his *Sentimental Lady* if he looked away?

    a. she would follow him

    b. she'd be cold to him

    c. she'd be gone

24. How do Peaches and Herb feel now that they're *Reunited*?

    a. as if their life is over

    b. so good

    c. as if they never left one another before

25. What does Stephen Bishop say people keep doing *On and On*?

    a. playing mind games with one another

    b. trying

    c. letting lies destroy their lives

26. In *Ruby (Don't Take Your Love to Town)*, how does Kenny Rogers describe his legs?

    a. bent and paralyzed

    b. sexy and inviting

    c. travel-worn with time

27. When does Dean Martin say *Everybody Loves Somebody*?

    a. when the pressure's on

    b. when love is in the air

    c. sometime

28. According to the Highwaymen, who helped *Michael* trim the sails?

    a. his dad

    b. the sister

    c. the oxen

29. In *Killing Me Softly With His Song,* what does Roberta Flack say was being told with his words?
   a. her whole life
   b. lies and more lies
   c. a sweet goodbye

30. In Bobby Vinton's *Blue Velvet,* what was bluer than velvet?
   a. her eyes
   b. his loneliness
   c. the ocean water

31. In *Chances Are,* Johnny Mathis says that if you think he loves you, how accurate is your hunch?
   a. it's not for him to say
   b. chances are awfully good
   c. it's an even chance

32. According to Pat Boone, how did you react whenever he cried because the tide had erased his *Love Letters in the Sand?*
   a. you held his hand
   b. you smiled tenderly
   c. you laughed

33. What do the Carpenters say birds do just to get *Close to You?*
   a. they fall down from the sky
   b. they sleep on your window sill
   c. they suddenly appear

34. In *Gentle on My Mind,* Glen Campbell says it's nice to know that what is always open to him?
   a. your heart
   b. your door
   c. your arms

35. According to O. C. Smith, if God didn't make the *Little Green Apples* then where doesn't it rain in the summertime?
  a. Phoenix
  b. Vancouver
  c. Indianapolis

36. In *Lipstick on Your Collar*, where did you leave Connie Francis all alone?
  a. at a movie
  b. at the beach
  c. at the record hop

37. Why does Christopher Cross have to *Ride Like the Wind*?
  a. to be free again
  b. to catch your love
  c. because you're an angel

38. In Mama Cass's *Dream a Little Dream of Me*, what do the night breezes seem to whisper?
  a. I love you
  b. I'm sorry
  c. it's cold out here

39. Even though they say *I'd Really Love to See You Tonight*, what don't England Dan and John Ford Coley want to do?
  a. meet your boyfriend
  b. see you again tomorrow
  c. move in

40. When what thing happens do the Platters say *Smoke Gets in Your Eyes*?
  a. when cigarettes fill the air
  b. when a lovely flame dies
  c. when you fall for a woman's lies

41. What did Barry Manilow do after *Mandy* came and gave without taking?
     a. he sent her away
     b. he begged her to stay
     c. he pledged his love to her

42. According to Sammy Davis, Jr., what does *The Candy Man* mix his candy with to make the world taste good?
     a. hope
     b. love
     c. sugar

43. In *She Believes in Me*, what does Kenny Rogers see in the night after stumbling to the kitchen?
     a. the girl of his dreams
     b. a faint glow
     c. his guitar

44. Along with a note, what else did Pat Boone find while at *Moody River*?
     a. your shoes
     b. a glove
     c. your picture

45. In *No Ordinary Love*, what did someone say to Sade?
     a. she needs to see a doctor
     b. you're good medicine
     c. a love like hers won't last

46. In *Do It to Me*, what happened when you put a spell on Lionel Richie?
     a. you made him your slave
     b. you set him free
     c. he lost his mind

47. In *It Takes Two*, what do Marvin Gaye and Kim Weston say two can make any place feel like?

a. being home
b. the Garden of Eden
c. a desert island

48. In *Breaking In a Brand New Broken Heart*, where does Connie Francis say she'll be if her friends should ask for her?
    a. in lonely land
    b. at a bar
    c. at home

49. What is Linda Ronstadt going to do for a *Long, Long Time*?
    a. cry
    b. hide in her dreams
    c. love you

50. What do the Platters count while awaiting *Twilight Time*?
    a. the stars in the sky
    b. the moments until you're with them
    c. the reasons they love you

BONUS QUIZ

1. Although it's over and done, what feeling of *Emotion* does Samantha Sang say still lives on and on?
    a. her love for you
    b. the heartache
    c. the memories

2. In *I Remember You*, what does Frank Ifield also remember with fondness?
    a. the times you cried
    b. the beach he and you walked along
    c. a distant bell

3. In *Wonderful, Wonderful* where are the Tymes standing with you, gazing at the earth and sky, when they turn to you and you melt into their arms?
   a. on their balcony
   b. on the top of a hill
   c. in paradise

4. According to the Highwaymen, in what state are the *Cotton Fields* located?
   a. Alabama
   b. Arkansas
   c. Louisiana

5. Although in *Tonight, You Belong to Me* you're apart from Patience and Prudence, what do they add?
   a. you're part of their heart
   b. they'll get you back
   c. you'll be sorry one day

6. In *My Heart Has a Mind of Its Own*, what did Connie Francis tell her heart?
   a. not to believe all those lies
   b. her love with you could never be
   c. not to pound so loudly whenever you walk by

7. In *It's Sad to Belong*, during what season did England Dan and John Ford Coley meet you?
   a. summer
   b. spring
   c. autumn

8. According to the Platters, when is a person *Enchanted*?
   a. when he touches a star
   b. when a lover calls
   c. after a good meal

9. In *I'm Sorry*, Brenda Lee says you told her that mistakes are part of ___.
   a. creation

    b. learning

    c. living

10. Bing Crosby and Grace Kelly say that *True Love* ____.

    a. lasts forever

    b. is a splendored thing

    c. is for dreamers

11. In *Banana Boat (Day-O)*, what does Harry Belafonte see that makes him want to go home?

    a. your face

    b. daylight

    c. no future

12. As a soldier away from home, what has been conspicuously absent for Bobby Vinton in *Mr. Lonely?*

    a. love

    b. a warm meal

    c. letters

13. In which season did Bobby Goldsboro's *Honey* leave this dimension?

    a. autumn

    b. winter

    c. spring

14. According to Pat Boone's *Speedy Gonzalez*, what does he need to get for his motor?

    a. a tune-up

    b. oil

    c. tortillas

15. According to Smokey and His Sister, who did the *Creators of Rain* create you for?

    a. them

    b. all the world to share

    c. yourself

16. In *Guantanamera*, what do the Sandpipers say they want to share before dying?

    a. the palms of their soul
    b. their pain and sorrow
    c. their dreams and hopes

17. In *I Just Called to Say I Love You*, how does Stevie Wonder describe the day?

    a. heaven sent
    b. cloudy and grey
    c. just an ordinary day

18. How much does Blue Magic say it'll cost to attend their *Sideshow*?

    a. it's free
    b. fifty cents
    c. one broken heart

19. In *Bluer Than Blue*, when Michael Johnson refers to himself as an empty room, what does he call you?

    a. the key
    b. the light
    c. the furniture

20. Before the start of which show did the Carpenters fall in love with their *Superstar*?

    a. the second
    b. the sixth
    c. the first

The Last Word

Rock and roll has gone through many stages of development since the first rockers picked up their guitars and invited a drummer to join the ensemble. Each stage is unique, yet each has contributed to the complexity and diversity of today's most successful bands. The fifties and sixties placed a great importance on the content of lyrics; the seventies seemed to stray from social consciousness and pursue an era of disco-dancing and outrageous fashions; and the eighties extracted the best of each of the previous three decades.

Where are we now? Listen to the latest CD tracks, and you may be surprised to find that the social consciousness is returning. Rap isn't "mindless," and the heavy metal rockers aren't simply "making noise." There is a vast wealth of cultural and philosophical knowledge being espoused in today's sounds. The immortality of the early years of rock and roll is a testament to the power and vision of youth. If one lesson is to be learned from all the carefully chosen—and truly representative—lyrics of the first twenty years of rock and roll, it is that we are now at the cutting edge of a new era of memorable rock lyrics. Just consider the music of the fifties, sixties, seventies, and the eighties as the legacy left to the rockers of the nineties. The history book of rock and roll is constantly being rewritten no matter what the year. So don't let the music pass you by—it's alive and well . . . and it will never die.

Answers

Elvis and the Early Rockers

QUIZ A

1. **a.** rabbit
2. **a.** if they try to change the melody
3. **c.** shapely hips
4. **b.** chicken
5. **b.** a little bit of lovin'
6. **b.** what they missed
7. **a.** if he's all alone
8. **b.** he was too young to vote
9. **c.** happiness
10. **a.** her mama
11. **a.** to stay
12. **a.** his seatbelt
13. **b.** after awhile, crocodile
14. **b.** as the prettiest green eyes anywhere
15. **b.** to say I'm sorry
16. **a.** make his dreams come true
17. **c.** Jack
18. **c.** joy
19. **a.** in the sands of Waikiki
20. **b.** rare and true
21. **c.** standing alone
22. **c.** sitting all alone
23. **a.** a pink carnation
24. **c.** blind

25. **a.** a glow in their heart
26. **c.** a bus
27. **b.** until the day he dies
28. **a.** 6'6"
29. **b.** his high school ring
30. **c.** they fell asleep at the movies
31. **c.** glue
32. **b.** twiddle his thumbs
33. **a.** tight dresses and high-heeled shoes
34. **c.** from up above
35. **b.** the pyramids
36. **a.** the newspaper
37. **a.** they aren't loved enough
38. **c.** he fell into it
39. **a.** their girlfriend
40. **c.** this was love
41. **a.** rock and roll
42. **c.** run your fingers through his hair
43. **b.** you
44. **b.** she breaks their hearts
45. **a.** he's done everything he can
46. **b.** dance
47. **a.** to show the world that he's yours
48. **c.** having fun
49. **c.** he kissed her again
50. **b.** it'll go down in history

QUIZ B

1. **c.** picture him there
2. **a.** they're dreaming their life away
3. **b.** Daisy
4. **c.** romance
5. **b.** by plane
6. **c.** 8:45
7. **a.** blow a fuse

8. **a.** talk about you
9. **a.** his world will end
10. **b.** romance
11. **b.** a Mexican girl
12. **c.** you
13. **c.** a love to share
14. **a.** all his dreams
15. **a.** you're going steady with nobody else
16. **b.** his baby's lips
17. **a.** across the floor
18. **a.** why you walked out on them
19. **c.** Tchaikovsky
20. **b.** thumbing for a ride
21. **c.** he dies
22. **c.** this morning
23. **c.** his heart
24. **c.** If he came back, which one would you choose?
25. **b.** her kisses
26. **b.** love them
27. **b.** wise men
28. **b.** a gunnysack
29. **a.** cold as ice
30. **a.** his face
31. **b.** take it to a private eye
32. **a.** May
33. **b.** the letters keep coming back
34. **b.** carefree devil eyes
35. **c.** a storm
36. **c.** his knee
37. **c.** the music
38. **a.** 1:00 A.M.
39. **c.** 8:00
40. **b.** where is she
41. **a.** walk
42. **b.** a Cadillac Coupe De Ville
43. **b.** ask to go steady

44. **a.** a darned good life
45. **b.** another mouth to feed
46. **c.** the touch of your hand
47. **a.** the trees
48. **b.** emptiness
49. **a.** ever since the world began
50. **a.** your love

BONUS QUIZ

1. **b.** 109°
2. **b.** 8:00 P.M.
3. **a.** he never thought he'd lose your love
4. **a.** living in paradise
5. **b.** to the happy hunting ground
6. **c.** you're the cutest little jailbird
7. **c.** Colonel Jackson
8. **c.** Clifton Clowers
9. **c.** he's in love with her
10. **c.** you'll ever know
11. **b.** a kiss
12. **b.** crying
13. **b.** one kiss
14. **c.** you'll care for him
15. **c.** chapter one
16. **c.** Johnny
17. **a.** Saturday
18. **a.** a heart full of tears
19. **a.** history
20. **c.** kiss him

Answers

The Beatles

QUIZ A

1. **c.** you love them, too
2. **a.** she knows you're not the hurtin' kind
3. **a.** that she's theirs
4. **c.** happy
5. **a.** if you don't take her out tonight
6. **b.** her man
7. **a.** seventeen
8. **b.** write home
9. **a.** because tomorrow may rain
10. **c.** that they'll always be in love with you
11. **c.** how much they really care
12. **b.** the way she moves
13. **b.** you're coming home
14. **a.** you can give them to the birds and bees
15. **b.** a diamond ring
16. **b.** let them know that she's theirs
17. **a.** love
18. **c.** take a walk
19. **b.** darling, I love you
20. **b.** Sunday driver
21. **c.** break their heart
22. **a.** make it better
23. **b.** the girl who drives them mad is going away
24. **a.** new

25. **b.** twenty
26. **c.** get by
27. **b.** all right
28. **a.** two feet small
29. **a.** Tucson
30. **a.** right now
31. **c.** call
32. **b.** help
33. **c.** troubles are here to stay
34. **a.** your door
35. **a.** Mother Mary
36. **c.** he enters from the pouring rain
37. **c.** the time and place when they met her
38. **a.** they're in love with someone else
39. **b.** they're not going to make it with anyone
40. **a.** you are near them
41. **c.** a little lovin'
42. **c.** leave you
43. **a.** they're in love
44. **a.** if you'd promise to be true
45. **b.** feed them
46. **b.** how she manages to make ends meet
47. **c.** a heart
48. **c.** pretend
49. **b.** birds
50. **b.** love

QUIZ B

1. **a.** that you'll understand
2. **b.** holding hands
3. **b.** you don't want their lovin' anymore
4. **c.** get her back
5. **b.** cry
6. **b.** that they would love everything you do

7. **a.** Father McKenzie
8. **b.** take you away
9. **c.** when they're lonely
10. **b.** next door
11. **b.** why you cry
12. **c.** BOAC
13. **c.** their baby
14. **a.** a Bible
15. **c.** kissing the lips they are missing
16. **c.** they don't know
17. **c.** how she manages to feed the rest
18. **a.** the world
19. **b.** wisdom
20. **c.** the world
21. **a.** disease
22. **b.** treat them the same way
23. **a.** the wave of her hand
24. **b.** a movie star
25. **a.** they belong to you
26. **c.** you weren't home
27. **c.** leave them
28. **a.** blue and lonely
29. **a.** she never tried to please them
30. **b.** an angel
31. **c.** in their mind
32. **c.** love
33. **c.** a state of mind
34. **a.** in the bath
35. **c.** since you'll be theirs
36. **b.** apologize to her
37. **c.** goodnight
38. **b.** you'll let them be your man
39. **a.** them
40. **b.** dance with another
41. **a.** the day they do love

42. **b.** diamond rings
43. **b.** love
44. **a.** they care
45. **a.** they'll be glad
46. **c.** she could never be free when they were around
47. **c.** like a dog
48. **b.** a paperback writer
49. **c.** their feet
50. **b.** they said something wrong

BONUS QUIZ

1. **c.** all the clowns
2. **a.** Lear
3. **a.** call on them
4. **c.** roses
5. **b.** to need her everywhere
6. **c.** cry
7. **a.** the only girl
8. **a.** not to step on their shoes
9. **c.** the mambo
10. **b.** the British
11. **b.** red
12. **c.** sad and lonely man
13. **b.** time
14. **a.** they saw you walk in your door
15. **b.** to them
16. **b.** show you the way
17. **c.** Ukraine
18. **b.** kill people
19. **a.** they'll be crucified
20. **c.** nothing is going to change their world

Answers

Rhythm and Blues / Soul

QUIZ A

1. **b.** Monday
2. **a.** San Francisco
3. **b.** three
4. **c.** Suzie
5. **b.** carousel
6. **b.** hold them tightly
7. **a.** when he's coming back
8. **a.** as a plaything
9. **a.** baby coach
10. **b.** a duchess
11. **a.** each other
12. **c.** when they need a hand to hold
13. **b.** beg
14. **b.** they're in love alone
15. **c.** another home
16. **b.** brand new
17. **a.** you to come over
18. **b.** 1965
19. **a.** what he is trying to do to her
20. **c.** a house and a family
21. **b.** anything wrong
22. **c.** disappointment
23. **b.** when a lovely flame dies

24. **c.** Billy-Joe
25. **a.** that all his girlfriend wants to do is use him
26. **b.** their mother
27. **c.** blue
28. **b.** perfume
29. **a.** them by your side
30. **b.** he's broke
31. **c.** she touches their hand
32. **c.** lonely
33. **c.** they held you
34. **b.** turn you some flips
35. **c.** loneliness
36. **a.** high-heeled shoes
37. **b.** lies
38. **a.** their boyfriend had found somebody new
39. **c.** the stars were shining bright
40. **c.** turn his back on the best friend
41. **a.** their heart
42. **c.** his life was filled with rain
43. **c.** don't forget who's taking you home
44. **c.** she just walks past them
45. **a.** a diamond ring
46. **a.** to fool the public
47. **b.** they'll be the vision of your happiness
48. **a.** it's only because opposites attract
49. **a.** James Brown
50. **a.** until their dying day

QUIZ B

1. **c.** because all advice ever got them was spending long and lonely nights
2. **b.** because tomorrow he's on his way
3. **c.** sunshine
4. **a.** because she doesn't want to
5. **b.** heaven

6. **c.** you never close your eyes anymore
7. **b.** love
8. **b.** proudly
9. **b.** sorrow
10. **a.** misery
11. **c.** he's half a man with no sense of pride
12. **c.** swinging with two chicks
13. **a.** joy
14. **c.** in her room
15. **a.** 12th Street and Vine
16. **a.** a card or letter saying their boyfriend is returning
17. **b.** Boney Maroney
18. **a.** how it is to be loved by you
19. **a.** it's like thunder and lightning
20. **a.** a gas
21. **b.** you
22. **a.** the sun goes down
23. **a.** they can't explain the tears they shed
24. **b.** the sun's rays
25. **c.** their baby
26 **b.** because of their obligations
27. **c.** whatever you want to do
28. **a.** a bee sting
29. **c.** what they're going through
30. **c.** average guy
31. **c.** the bag they're in
32. **a.** making romance
33. **b.** toy
34. **b.** summer
35. **a.** afraid
36. **a.** wavy
37. **c.** they're going to love you
38. **c.** at the candy store
39. **a.** he takes a trip around the world
40. **c.** getting to her

41. **b.** he was thinking of you
42. **c.** his eyes
43. **b.** Frank and Jim
44. **b.** drag
45. **c.** his love
46. **c.** you do
47. **c.** marry her
48. **a.** come home
49. **b.** love's sweet melody
50. **a.** how much they love you

BONUS QUIZ

1. **c.** pet
2. **c.** they believe they're falling in love
3. **b.** whenever you're near
4. **b.** working
5. **a.** pain
6. **a.** lovers
7. **c.** 5:00 A.M.
8. **b.** moment's pleasure
9. **c.** so slowly
10. **b.** a fantasy
11. **c.** Los Angeles
12. **a.** boyfriend
13. **b.** alone
14. **a.** other people's property
15. **c.** digging a ditch
16. **a.** when he touches a star
17. **c.** Billy
18. **a.** at McDonald's
19. **b.** take out the papers and the trash
20. **a.** the women get jealous

Answers

American Rock: The First Two Decades

QUIZ A

1. **c.** bullfrogs
2. **b.** misery
3. **a.** a summer shower
4. **c.** Boston
5. **b.** Stingrays and Jaguars
6. **a.** human respect
7. **a.** only half as much as tomorrow
8. **a.** a summer's night
9. **b.** a ship
10. **b.** change their mind
11. **b.** by the riverside
12. **c.** he won't live to see tomorrow
13. **c.** teardrops
14. **b.** $5
15. **a.** cantaloupe
16. **c.** paradise
17. **b.** Sunday
18. **c.** turn the radio volume up
19. **c.** her huggin', kissin', and lovin'
20. **a.** a killer
21. **b.** the time was right to follow her
22. **a.** you've got to make the morning last
23. **b.** walk upon the land

24. **a.** Johnny
25. **b.** chicken and dumplings
26. **b.** be close at hand
27. **a.** a penthouse
28. **c.** you've got nothing to lose
29. **b.** pray
30. **c.** one woman
31. **b.** love
32. **a.** punch
33. **b.** nothing to lose
34. **b.** your mama said you cried in bed
35. **a.** gentle
36. **a.** their bundle of joy
37. **b.** it's driving them insane
38. **a.** a chance to hold you in their arms
39. **a.** a lifetime
40. **c.** 5:00 P.M.
41. **b.** give her love to them
42. **c.** for the summer
43. **b.** they get so timid and shy
44. **a.** faded
45. **c.** her good looks
46. **b.** she took it off her finger
47. **c.** reach your goal
48. **a.** Johnny and Judy
49. **c.** behave
50. **b.** dreams that can't come true

QUIZ B

1. **c.** lucky
2. **a.** in a café
3. **b.** the sounds of the city
4. **c.** their grandfather
5. **c.** the sun
6. **c.** take them for a ride

7. **a.** the Lord
8. **b.** that you'll never leave him
9. **c.** if she wants to go to see a movie
10. **a.** love
11. **a.** a ragged sweatshirt
12. **a.** that you love him
13. **b.** it brought him to you
14. **b.** kind
15. **a.** get married
16. **b.** Have you got cheating on your mind?
17. **b.** he doesn't know that she exists
18. **b.** Jesus
19. **c.** their car
20. **b.** she's gone away
21. **b.** you stood there, grinning
22. **b.** to the ground
23. **a.** perfume
24. **b.** the sounds
25. **c.** Rosie
26. **c.** beware
27. **b.** they couldn't get much higher
28. **a.** another boy has taken you from him
29. **c.** the city
30. **c.** no fun anymore
31. **a.** it starts
32. **c.** hadn't been done before
33. **a.** fifteen cents
34. **a.** a lecture
35. **a.** not so hard
36. **c.** he'll mistreat her
37. **b.** the clock
38. **c.** take care of the one they love
39. **b.** what the future would be if she stayed with them
40. **b.** a coffeehouse
41. **a.** two

42. **c.** tears
43. **c.** two to one
44. **a.** that you were their friend
45. **c.** until his dreaming comes true
46. **a.** by some other boy's name
47. **b.** cry
48. **a.** only love can mend it again
49. **b.** flirt with you
50. **b.** why they must say goodbye

BONUS QUIZ

1. **a.** blue
2. **c.** a racehorse
3. **b.** when they were her chosen one
4. **b.** Betty Lou and Peggy Sue
5. **a.** along the sand
6. **c.** the hippies
7. **b.** she was colorblind
8. **c.** you're never out of his sight
9. **c.** a place to hide
10. **b.** Tommy
11. **a.** the U.S. Army
12. **a.** what their name was
13. **a.** the point of a gun
14. **c.** shingaling and bugaloo
15. **b.** your love
16. **a.** chrome-reversed
17. **b.** dance to the Surfer Stomp
18. **c.** Malibu
19. **b.** a symphony
20. **c.** seven

Answers

The British Invasion

QUIZ A

1. **a.** you'll part
2. **c.** to love each other
3. **a.** by changing horses
4. **c.** always low
5. **a.** to spend their life with you
6. **b.** barroom queen
7. **a.** take your heart away
8. **a.** New Orleans
9. **c.** they're in love with you
10. **c.** the things he'd been dreaming of
11. **c.** intuition and smell
12. **c.** geometry
13. **b.** Where is she?
14. **a.** on the corner of 34th and Vine
15. **b.** you'll come running back to them
16. **a.** take a look at you
17. **c.** the nighttime
18. **a.** break up
19. **a.** there ain't no use in tryin'
20. **c.** a snail
21. **a.** you're the one they love
22. **b.** fingers and toes
23. **c.** the trees
24. **a.** that their eyes still see

25. **b.** there's a way to do every little thing
26. **c.** how white their shirts should be
27. **a.** being lazy
28. **b.** let them down
29. **c.** they'd do it to you
30. **b.** whose intentions are good
31. **b.** you're not to blame
32. **c.** a bachelor
33. **b.** her love belongs to them
34. **a.** show you where it's at
35. **c.** because of their pride
36. **c.** when you're without love
37. **a.** when they woke up this morning
38. **b.** her loneliness
39. **b.** all over the world
40. **c.** a Siamese cat
41. **b.** found somebody to take his place
42. **c.** a kiss
43. **b.** they left their girlfriend standing on her own
44. **c.** simple
45. **a.** the bossa nova
46. **c.** no one
47. **b.** by your side
48. **a.** despair
49. **b.** seasick
50. **c.** ninety-ninth

QUIZ B

1. **b.** you can do what you want
2. **a.** the morning
3. **b.** last night
4. **c.** they both disagreed
5. **c.** it's gonna be a drag
6. **b.** during a hurricane

7. **a.** she makes their heart sing
8. **a.** their own secret cares
9. **c.** dream of them
10. **b.** an umbrella
11. **a.** in the daytime
12. **a.** the tired eyes
13. **a.** midnight
14. **b.** look the other way
15. **b.** goodbye
16. **c.** evening
17. **b.** they're together with their girlfriend
18. **c.** fun
19. **b.** you've told them you want to leave them
20. **a.** sable
21. **c.** Who's your daddy?
22. **c.** last night
23. **b.** brilliant
24. **a.** listen to their advice
25. **b.** his window
26. **c.** lock them away
27. **b.** down in the hollow
28. **a.** your one and only
29. **b.** cry
30. **c.** no one
31. **a.** Liverpool
32. **c.** in the city
33. **a.** Will they be bolder than today?
34. **a.** let her give her heart to him
35. **b.** broken
36. **c.** by your side
37. **a.** colors
38. **a.** perhaps they'll die there
39. **b.** their dreams
40. **a.** love you
41. **c.** the whole world started laughing

42. b. conservatively
43. c. nothing
44. b. shadows
45. b. she changes with every new day
46. a. war
47. b. 5'4"
48. a. reach the sky
49. b. from both sides
50. c. home

BONUS QUIZ

1. a. Ravi Shankar
2. a. a bomb
3. b. a crystal ball
4. a. you and me
5. c. the music
6. b. find a man
7. c. bad
8. b. striptease
9. a. their girlfriend walking with another guy
10. b. the rain falling upon the window pane
11. c. sing
12. a. your nose
13. c. begins to crumble
14. c. ten
15. a. twenty-five cents
16. b. strange
17. c. always low
18. b. the jerk
19. a. to keep you satisfied
20. c. the promised land

Answers

American Pop

QUIZ A

1. **c.** big brother
2. **a.** by surrey
3. **c.** take your place
4. **b.** rain
5. **b.** like she's going to lose her mind
6. **a.** be just like his dad
7. **a.** two
8. **c.** junkyard dog
9. **b.** west
10. **c.** a county fair
11. **b.** a Chevy
12. **c.** how much you love him
13. **a.** the Jordan river
14. **b.** go to sleep and dream again
15. **c.** start something new
16. **b.** he loves you
17. **c.** in that way, they won't ever fight
18. **b.** nothing seems to fit
19. **b.** a thousand
20. **a.** cry
21. **c.** in a wagon
22. **a.** flashing red lights
23. **b.** the writing on the wall
24. **c.** crawl

25. **a.** they like it
26. **a.** that you'll always be the same person that he's known
27. **a.** change the way things are
28. **a.** inside yourself
29. **c.** their lady's eyes
30. **a.** soul
31. **c.** his life was filled with rain
32. **a.** his heart
33. **b.** weak
34. **a.** he went away
35. **b.** it doesn't spoil the whole bunch
36. **a.** you
37. **b.** they'll burn inside of her
38. **a.** walking hand in hand with one he loves
39. **c.** nobody
40. **c.** walks the wire
41. **b.** loneliness
42. **a.** May
43. **b.** he wants you
44. **b.** criticize him
45. **a.** keep it inside
46. **a.** his bodyguard
47. **b.** without you by her side
48. **b.** her heart out
49. **a.** your body
50. **b.** it's the best feeling he's ever known

QUIZ B

1. **c.** only half as much as tomorrow
2. **a.** his wife
3. **b.** Jesus
4. **c.** love you
5. **a.** faults
6. **b.** take a ride in their balloon

7. **a.** February
8. **c.** boss
9. **a.** they are expressed in their songs
10. **b.** a yacht
11. **b.** Louie Miller
12. **a.** in love with him
13. **c.** loneliness calls
14. **a.** they're just about to die
15. **a.** one night
16. **b.** macho man
17. **c.** in your car
18. **a.** we're all carried along
19. **c.** the earth
20. **b.** the world will be a better place
21. **a.** Baton Rouge
22. **c.** survive
23. **b.** cheating on her
24. **c.** your love
25. **b.** that she's a fool who's willing to wait
26. **a.** she starts to glow
27. **a.** a moth to the flame
28. **c.** Blue Boy
29. **b.** darkness
30. **b.** live
31. **b.** a man that's true
32. **c.** they won't fall again
33. **a.** sleep on it
34. **b.** something died deep inside
35. **a.** a turnip green
36. **a.** it turns him off
37. **c.** destiny
38. **a.** they are our future
39. **c.** things he can't do
40. **b.** wrapped in your arms
41. **a.** walk all over you
42. **a.** three thousand

43. **a.** blue
44. **c.** kiss your lips
45. **c.** that there was a party going on
46. **b.** his ex-friend Ray
47. **c.** Waterloo
48. **b.** light their fire
49. **a.** tonight
50. **c.** on the ceiling

BONUS QUIZ

1. **b.** the rhythm of her sigh
2. **a.** living
3. **c.** he's not a fool for them
4. **b.** driving in a car
5. **c.** roses and his dreams
6. **b.** December
7. **c.** Los Angeles
8. **c.** it's in the seventh house
9. **c.** eighteen years
10. **c.** December
11. **b.** a mint
12. **c.** take her in his arms
13. **a.** a peppered sprout
14. **a.** makes promises she can't keep
15. **c.** on the street
16. **b.** she doesn't want it
17. **a.** the neon lights
18. **a.** in the arms of someone else
19. **c.** How can she be strong?
20. **c.** souvenirs

Answers

Dance / Party Rock

QUIZ A

1. **c.** cool
2. **c.** they tear the house down
3. **c.** squeeze him
4. **a.** in the tunnel of love
5. **b.** he was too tough
6. **b.** your hips
7. **a.** her looks
8. **b.** they don't know
9. **c.** their minds and souls
10. **b.** across the floor
11. **a.** they're the best in town
12. **a.** danger and excitement
13. **b.** their love
14. **c.** nobody but you
15. **a.** on the dance floor
16. **b.** tonight
17. **a.** play by rules
18. **c.** treat her right
19. **b.** a change of scenery
20. **a.** bird
21. **a.** take his girl out on a date
22. **b.** they are sharp as a pistol
23. **a.** learning the ABC's
24. **a.** eighty

25. **c.** they're too busy singing to put anybody down
26. **a.** if you're going to love her forever
27. **a.** love
28. **b.** leave you alone and let you and them be together
29. **a.** get up
30. **a.** as soon as they started to move
31. **c.** your arms
32. **c.** only the sexy people
33. **a.** they can dance
34. **b.** one hundred stories
35. **c.** funky
36. **b.** she turned down the speaker
37. **a.** a chick in slacks
38. **b.** they couldn't dance
39. **c.** Dracula
40. **b.** across the track
41. **a.** her eyes
42. **a.** the Sunset Strip
43. **c.** he doesn't want to go
44. **a.** you can get kissed
45. **b.** a raven
46. **c.** make love to you
47. **b.** a dinosaur
48. **c.** Camp Granada
49. **a.** you'
50. **b.** a Rambler

QUIZ B

1. **a.** him
2. **a.** you're by her side
3. **b.** 6:00
4. **a.** a flower girl
5. **b.** so good
6. **a.** the flame was just for him

7. **c.** on the floor
8. **a.** got a groove
9. **c.** her sisters
10. **c.** let the well run dry
11. **b.** boogie on the floor
12. **c.** they're not sure of a love there is no cure for
13. **a.** the twist, stomp, and mashed potato
14. **c.** Houston
15. **a.** the hully gully
16. **c.** an ugly girl
17. **b.** candy girl
18. **a.** Merry Christmas!
19. **a.** fight
20. **b.** a new dance craze
21. **c.** dance and make love
22. **b.** that he was losing you
23. **c.** to you
24. **a.** if you'll be his girl
25. **b.** he doesn't know how it started
26. **a.** that they feel so good
27. **c.** they don't mind
28. **c.** a canoe
29. **b.** they're your loving man
30. **c.** it's so good
31. **a.** the rent is late
32. **a.** the honeysuckle
33. **b.** South Street
34. **c.** the right words to say
35. **a.** public scenes
36. **c.** exchange them
37. **b.** when they play the music tight
38. **a.** they're a woman's man
39. **c.** everybody
40. **a.** they love you
41. **c.** love
42. **a.** spread your feet

43. **b.** he makes them feel so good
44. **a.** the world
45. **b.** home
46. **c.** pony and twist
47. **b.** with a space-age design
48. **c.** you will never grow old
49. **a.** dance
50. **c.** 45th Street

BONUS QUIZ

1. **b.** Long Tall Sally
2. **b.** Fred
3. **a.** A-E-I-O-U
4. **b.** leave your cares behind
5. **c.** halt
6. **c.** a bowl of soup
7. **a.** red, blue, and green
8. **b.** percussion
9. **a.** San Francisco
10. **a.** rescue him
11. **b.** a bird
12. **b.** dance
13. **b.** Daddy G
14. **c.** Saturday
15. **c.** scared
16. **c.** he better shape up
17. **a.** staying home
18. **c.** nine years old
19. **b.** like a Boy Scout
20. **b.** 4:30

Answers

Contemporary American Rock

QUIZ A

1. **c.** lonely
2. **b.** love
3. **a.** a helluva band
4. **c.** take you higher
5. **a.** the rains
6. **b.** good times
7. **a.** the old man's money
8. **a.** satisfy every fantasy you think of
9. **c.** you might have found somebody new
10. **b.** like a son
11. **a.** show how you feel
12. **b.** you've been messing around
13. **b.** her letter
14. **a.** love you
15. **b.** a dreamer
16. **c.** whiter than white
17. **a.** dancing
18. **c.** a tidal wave
19. **c.** make it up to you
20. **b.** Jeremiah
21. **c.** every raging wind that comes
22. **a.** when you can't be with the one you love
23. **a.** life is for living
24. **b.** party down

25. **a.** a piece of grass
26. **c.** it was like slow motion
27. **b.** living in the jungle
28. **c.** real
29. **a.** into shape
30. **c.** a game in their mind
31. **a.** Saturday
32. **b.** your attention
33. **a.** underneath the train
34. **c.** touch their bodies
35. **a.** the thrill of living is gone
36. **c.** Romeo and Juliet
37. **a.** Marianne
38. **b.** made love for the first time
39. **b.** hopeless
40. **b.** wild and free
41. **a.** in worn-out shoes and baggy pants
42. **c.** use it
43. **b.** it makes them money
44. **a.** nothing's wrong
45. **a.** there'll be peace
46. **b.** run away
47. **b.** a black sedan
48. **c.** when he dies
49. **c.** a love like this
50. **b.** he had her

QUIZ B

1. **b.** when you want to let a feeling show
2. **c.** playing cards with the boys
3. **a.** it goes on
4. **a.** in his pocket
5. **b.** Sunday
6. **c.** the city they live in
7. **a.** the light

8. **b.** childhood memories
9. **a.** he blows her mind
10. **a.** in Japan
11. **b.** find a job
12. **a.** you're both never satisfied
13. **b.** roll with the punches
14. **a.** nothing that he didn't already have
15. **c.** let them know
16. **c.** you come home late
17. **b.** almost anything you want them to
18. **b.** your face
19. **a.** on the radio
20. **c.** hold on
21. **c.** make a devil out of him
22. **b.** you're going to please them
23. **a.** get high awhile
24. **c.** a crazy kiss
25. **a.** play
26. **c.** someone new to talk to
27. **a.** a fantasy
28. **c.** a mountain stream
29. **b.** it's a place to get away from it all
30. **c.** turn you down
31. **a.** the poet in their heart
32. **b.** it's easier than dealing with the pain
33. **c.** black
34. **c.** do the New Kids dance
35. **a.** that isn't going to get them anywhere
36. **c.** making love to her
37. **a.** inside a room
38. **b.** their partner
39. **b.** them
40. **c.** have a good time
41. **a.** it keeps slipping into the future
42. **c.** the hangman
43. **a.** your arms

44. **b.** on the line, anytime
45. **b.** in the spotlight
46. **c.** so you can't see their tears
47. **b.** because love isn't always on time
48. **a.** then why can't they paint you
49. **b.** he wears them
50. **a.** pain

BONUS QUIZ

1. **c.** the moments they share with you
2. **a.** Bobby
3. **c.** the ticking of the clock
4. **a.** how they could have let you so down
5. **a.** somebody to take their place
6. **b.** Imagine that, me working for you!
7. **c.** never play the game too long
8. **a.** lay them on the table
9. **b.** as a dead-man's town
10. **c.** your body
11. **a.** Virgil Caine
12. **b.** Frank Zappa and the Mothers
13. **c.** he spoke
14. **b.** in a railway station
15. **c.** a golden oldie
16. **b.** the expanding man
17. **a.** a breakdown
18. **c.** Ricky
19. **b.** it always wins
20. **b.** Western inflation

Answers

UK Contemporary Rock

QUIZ A

1. **b.** Chevy
2. **a.** fire
3. **c.** never stop
4. **c.** watching you
5. **c.** you're never quite the same
6. **b.** seventeen
7. **a.** get back to her
8. **c.** anything you need
9. **b.** start again
10. **b.** Glenn Miller
11. **c.** all that glitters is gold
12. **c.** in the middle of the night
13. **a.** they were wrong
14. **b.** the weather
15. **c.** they love you
16. **b.** memories
17. **b.** a dreamer
18. **a.** their love
19. **c.** turn on her red light
20. **a.** listened long enough to you
21. **b.** leave the kids alone
22. **a.** ride the skies
23. **b.** jump off
24. **c.** how he feels

25. **b.** fools
26. **a.** dance
27. **a.** shoot the deputy
28. **b.** love you twice as much
29. **a.** rival
30. **b.** a pill
31. **c.** they're so raw
32. **a.** in a day or two
33. **c.** chicks
34. **a.** more, more, more
35. **c.** on the sand
36. **a.** tattered and torn
37. **b.** people think they're crazy
38. **c.** it takes so long
39. **a.** to be abused
40. **b.** someone to show them
41. **c.** be gone
42. **a.** that it was upside down
43. **c.** what's wrong with that?
44. **c.** only fools rush in
45. **b.** sometimes they don't make the man
46. **a.** drink or smoke
47. **b.** she gave them breakfast
48. **b.** why you and they should get along so awfully
49. **c.** in her apartment
50. **a.** smile

QUIZ B

1. **b.** the fever
2. **c.** the same thing
3. **b.** cheat a friend
4. **c.** he's being used
5. **b.** pain
6. **a.** to be left alone
7. **c.** black as the dark night

8. **a.** go out with your fancy friends
9. **c.** look at you
10. **b.** falling in love
11. **c.** on the sun
12. **a.** hunt for you
13. **a.** something they can remember her by
14. **c.** Saturday
15. **c.** she doesn't know his name
16. **a.** sort it out
17. **c.** it may not last
18. **a.** join the human race
19. **b.** scratch the surface
20. **c.** a rolling stone
21. **a.** fine
22. **b.** take a look at her
23. **b.** going out
24. **a.** 666
25. **b.** Major Thom
26. **a.** a child
27. **a.** that you're in love with them
28. **c.** in a doorway
29. **c.** the law
30. **b.** what happiness really meant
31. **a.** let him know
32. **c.** because he can't remember
33. **b.** Have you ever wondered why?
34. **b.** sorrow and pain
35. **c.** Spain
36. **c.** knowledge
37. **b.** would you know his name
38. **c.** hit you
39. **a.** balloons
40. **a.** across the bridge
41. **c.** a bullet
42. **a.** no one can say they didn't try
43. **a.** that the morning has come so soon

44. **c.** spread her wings
45. **b.** Billy
46. **a.** you're in the world
47. **c.** the love
48. **a.** someone was shot
49. **b.** rock the place to the ground
50. **b.** a bed of nails

BONUS QUIZ

1. **b.** in Soho
2. **b.** it has just begun
3. **a.** a Bible
4. **a.** by row boat
5. **c.** thinking of the future
6. **b.** steel
7. **c.** the tournament
8. **b.** they fought the Redskins
9. **c.** because he's got a daytime job
10. **a.** she slapped Johnny's face
11. **b.** Christ
12. **a.** make Neanderthal love
13. **c.** fall to their knees and pray
14. **c.** ever since she's been gone
15. **c.** how to leave you
16. **b.** pouring out his heart for prosperity
17. **b.** on your window sill
18. **a.** run every test from A to Z
19. **c.** horses and women
20. **a.** in the midnight sea

Answers

Easy Listening

QUIZ A

1. **b.** who really loves you
2. **a.** because of summer vacation
3. **c.** the jasmine
4. **b.** their roof has a hole in it
5. **b.** hold you tight
6. **a.** that someone waits for her
7. **b.** it's because you're around
8. **a.** love
9. **c.** he'd rather hurt you honestly than mislead you with a lie
10. **b.** you are the magnet, he is steel
11. **c.** on the sand
12. **b.** how much you care
13. **b.** you've got leaving on your mind
14. **a.** the more you make them see
15. **a.** he's been in love with you
16. **b.** forget her
17. **c.** their love would end this way
18. **a.** when he looks in your eyes
19. **c.** the thought of you
20. **a.** in the wine
21. **b.** a horse and carriage
22. **c.** better
23. **b.** anything
24. **a.** dancing to the jitterbug

25. a. cling to it
26. c. the thrill is gone
27. b. their love
28. c. hope to carry on
29. a. watching all the girls go by
30. b. because dreamin' will make you his
31. c. count your money
32. b. the cable cars
33. c. joy
34. c. there will come a day when they'll walk along side of him
35. a. letters
36. b. you close your eyes
37. b. someone you love
38. b. yesterday morning
39. c. get in shape
40. a. let love depart
41. c. straight ahead
42. c. she's in love
43. a. leaving
44. a. he belongs to someone else
45. b. twenty-one
46. a. Santa Catalina
47. a. don't just love any man
48. c. kindness
49. a. dream
50. b. forever

QUIZ B

1. b. how long he'll love you
2. a. the cake
3. a. Old Man Trouble
4. a. I love you
5. c. his little angel
6. b. say goodbye

7. **a.** everyone
8. **b.** living
9. **c.** rising
10. **c.** you think he's fine
11. **a.** the rainbow
12. **a.** that you'll always care
13. **c.** lie awake all night long
14. **a.** Kingston
15. **b.** next to him
16. **a.** keep their love out of sight
17. **c.** the moon and New York City
18. **c.** in her yearbook
19. **b.** you've found someone new
20. **a.** he breaks her heart in two
21. **c.** lost on a desert
22. **a.** believe in it
23. **c.** she'd be gone
24. **b.** so good
25. **b.** trying
26. **a.** bent and paralyzed
27. **c.** sometime
28. **b.** the sister
29. **a.** her whole life
30. **a.** her eyes
31. **b.** chances are awfully good
32. **c.** you laughed
33. **c.** they suddenly appear
34. **b.** your door
35. **c.** Indianapolis
36. **c.** at the record hop
37. **a.** to be free again
38. **a.** I love you
39. **c.** move in
40. **b.** when a lovely flame dies
41. **a.** he sent her away
42. **b.** love

43. **c.** his guitar
44. **b.** a glove
45. **c.** a love like hers won't last
46. **b.** you set him free
47. **a.** being home
48. **c.** at home
49. **c.** love you
50. **b.** the moments until you're with them

BONUS QUIZ

1. **b.** the heartache
2. **c.** a distant bell
3. **b.** on the top of a hill
4. **c.** Louisiana
5. **a.** you're part of their heart
6. **b.** her love with you could never be
7. **b.** spring
8. **a.** when he touches a star
9. **a.** creation
10. **a.** lasts forever
11. **b.** daylight
12. **c.** letters
13. **c.** spring
14. **c.** tortillas
15. **a.** them
16. **a.** the palms of their soul
17. **c.** just an ordinary day
18. **b.** fifty cents
19. **b.** the light
20. **a.** the second

About the Author

Presley Love has long been a music enthusiast. He joined the Byrds fan club in the sixties and maintained allegiance to the rock movement throughout his high school years. Before graduating from Kalani High School in Honolulu, Hawaii, he surveyed the entire student body and complied a "Top 100" survey of favorite songs. He graduated cum laude from the University of Hawaii, writing a hundred-page analysis of the words of Bob Dylan for his honors thesis.

Mr. Love continues to keep up-to-date with the latest trends, teaching in high school as well as deejaying special music events in Hawaii in his spare time. He is presently working on a rock titles trivia collection.

Books For Rock Fans
From Carol Publishing Group

The Art & Music of John Lennon, by John Robertson   paperback $12.95   (#51438)

The Best Rock 'n Roll Records of All Time: A Fan's Guide to the Stuff You Love by Jimmy Guterman   paperback $12.95   (#51325)

<u>Books From Citadel Underground:
Classic Books of the Counterculture—
Challenging Consensus Reality Since 1990</u>

Bob Dylan: Portraits From the Singer's Early Years by DanielKramer
oversized paperback $16.95   (#51224)

Conversations With the Dead: The Grateful Dead Interview Book by David Gans
paperback $14.95   (#51223)

Rock Folk: Portraits From the Rock 'n Roll Pantheon by Michael Lydon; introduction by Peter Guralnick   paperback $9.95 (#51206)

Turn It Up! (I can't hear the words): Singer/Songwriters, Then & Now by Bob Sarlin
paperback $9.95 (#51315)

Wanted Man: In Search of Bob Dylan Edited by John Bauldie
paperback $9.95 (#51266)
(call or write for a FREE
Citadel Underground brochure)

Broken Record: The Inside Story of the Grammy Awards by Henry Schipper
hardcover $17.95   (#72104)

Dark Star: The Roy Orbison Story by Ellis Amburn   hardcover $18.95   (#40518)

ELVIS! The Last Word by Sandra Choron & Bob Oskam   paperback $ 8.95   (#51280)

The Eric Clapton Scrapbook by Marc Roberty
oversized paperback $16.95   (#51454)

The Howard Stern Book: An Unauthorized, Unabashed, Uncensored Fan's Guide by Jim Cegielski; foreword by "Grampa" Al Lewis
paperback $12.95   (#51505)

The Jimmy Buffett Scrapbook by Mark Humphrey with Harris Lewine
oversized paperback $17.95   (#51461)

The Last Days of John Lennon: A Personal Memoir by Fred Seaman
hardcover $19.95   (#72084)

The Many Lives of Elton John by Susan Crimp & Patricia Burstein   hardcover $19.95   (#72111)

Rock Lyrics Quiz Book by Presley Love
paperback $10.95   (#51527)

Rock Names: From ABBA to ZZ Top—How Rock Bands Got Their Names by Adam Dolgins   paperback $9.95   (#51363)

Rockonomics: The Money Behind the Music by Marc Eliot
paperback $12.95   (#51457)

The Show Must Go On: The Life of Freddie Mercury by Rick Sky
paperback $10.95   (#51506)

Simon & Garfunkel: Old Friends—A Dual Biography by Joseph Morella & Patricia Barey   hardcover $19.95   (#72089)

Taxi: The Harry Chapin Story by Peter M. Coan   paperback $14.95 (#40513)

The Worst Rock 'n Roll Records of All Time: A Fan's Guide to the Stuff You Love to Hate by Jimmy Guterman & Owen O'Donnell
paperback $14.95   (#51231)

Prices subject to change;
books subject to availability